THE ORCHARD
(AFTER CHEKHOV)

The Orchard
(After Chekhov)

Sarena Parmar

The Orchard (After Chekhov)
first published 2020 by Scirocco Drama
An imprint of J. Gordon Shillingford Publishing Inc.
© 2020 Sarena Parmar

Scirocco Drama Editor: Glenda MacFarlane

Cover design by Doowah Design
Author photo by David Cooper.

5 lines on page 73 are from *Selected Poems by Rabindranath Tagore*, edited and translated by William Radice (Penguin Books, 1986). (Penguin Books Ltd, 1994). Translation, Introduction, Notes and Glossary copyright © William Radice, 1985. 1987, 1993, 1994

Printed and bound in Canada on 100% post-consumer recycled paper. We acknowledge the financial support of the Manitoba Arts Council and The Canada Council for the Arts for our publishing program.

All rights reserved. No part of this book may be reproduced, for any reason, by any means, without the permission of the publisher. This play is fully protected under the copyright laws of Canada and all other countries of the Copyright Union and is subject to royalty. Changes to the text are expressly forbidden without written consent of the author. Rights to produce, film, record in whole or in part, in any medium or in any language, by any group, amateur or professional, are retained by the author.

Production inquiries, please contact:
Playwrights Guild of Canada
401 Richmond Street West, Suite 350
Toronto, ON M5V 3A8
416-703-0201
info@playwrightsguild.ca
www.playwrightsguild.ca

Library and Archives Canada Cataloguing in Publication

Title: The orchard (after Chekhov) / Sarena Parmar.
Names: Parmar, Sarena, author. | adaptation of (work): Chekhov, Anton Pavlovich, 1860-1904.
 Vishnevyĭ sad.
Description: A play. | Adaptation of Chekhov's The cherry orchard.
Identifiers: Canadiana 20200189115 | ISBN 9781927922606 (softcover)
Classification: LCC PS8631.A7668 O73 2020 | DDC C812/.6—dc23

J. Gordon Shillingford Publishing
P.O. Box 86, RPO Corydon Avenue, Winnipeg, MB Canada R3M 3S3

For my family.

Table of Contents

Author Bio 9
Acknowledgements 10
Production History 11
Foreword
BY GUILLERMO VERDECCHIA 13
Production Notes 16
Characters 18

The Orchard
(After Chekhov) 21

Afterword: Re-imagining Canadian History
BY SARENA PARMAR 129
Farmers by Faith:
Following the Migrations of Sikh Cultivators
BY JAGDEESH MANN 134
Translation vs Transportation:
Can Chekhov Only Speak Russian?
BY TIM CARROLL 138
Journey of the Kishu-Ben Dialect:
Alternate Japanese Translation
TRANSLATED BY CHUCK TASAKA,
MAYU TAKASAKI AND CAROLYN NAKAGAWA 141

Sarena Parmar

Sarena Parmar is a Canadian actor and playwright. She is an acting graduate of the National Theatre School and the Birmingham Conservatory for Classical Theatre (Stratford Festival). As an actor, Sarena has worked across the country in theatre, film and TV.

The Orchard (After Chekhov) is her first full-length play. It premiered at the Shaw Festival in 2018, making Parmar the first South Asian playwright produced in the festival's history. She is also a recipient of the Elliot Hayes Playwright Development Fund awarded by the Stratford Festival.

Sarena grew up on her family orchard in Kelowna, British Columbia. She now lives in Toronto, splitting her time between acting and writing.

Acknowledgements

Thank you to Nina Lee Aquino for her belief in me as an artist, and as the first supporter of this play.

The Orchard (After Chekhov) has had a long road to production. It would not have been possible without Cahoots Theatre and Diaspora Dialogues. Thank you to Marjorie Chan, Guillermo Verdecchia, Tim Carroll and Ravi Jain for championing this ambitious play.

A special thank you to Coralee Miller and the Sncewips Heritage Museum for their guidance and generosity.

Production History

The Orchard (*After Chekhov*) premiered at the Shaw Festival in Niagara-on-the-Lake, Ontario, on June 23rd 2018, with the following cast and creative team. Programmed by Artistic Director Tim Carroll.

> LOVELEEN......................... Pamela Sinha
> GURJIT.............................. Sanjay Talwar
> ANNIE............................... Sarena Parmar
> BARBRA .... Krystal Kiran
> KESUR .... David Adams
> MICHAEL........................... Jeff Meadows
> PETER................................ Shawn Ahmed
> YASH .... Andrew Lawrie
> YEBI................................... Kelly Wong
> DONNA/BOY .... Rong Fu
> CHARLIE............................ Jani Lauzon
> PAUL .... Neil Barclay

Directed by Ravi Jain
Assistant Director: Diana Donnelly
Set and Costume Design: Camellia Koo
Lighting Design: André du Toit
Original Music and Sound Design: Debashis Sinha
Stage Manager: Andrea Schurman
Cultural Consultant: Gurpreet Chana
Fight Direction: John Stead
Dramaturgy: Guillermo Verdecchia
Punjabi Translation: Gurpreet Chana
Japanese Translation: Aya Ogawa

A second production of *The Orchard* (*After Chekhov*) opened at the Arts Club Theatre Company in Vancouver BC on March 27th 2019, with the following cast and creative team. Programmed by Artistic Director, Ashlie Corcoran, in her inaugural season.

LOVELEEN	Laara Sadiq
GURJIT	Munish Sharma
ANNIE	Risha Nanda
BARBRA	Adele Noronha
KESUR	Parm Soor
MICHAEL	Andrew Cownden
PETER	Nadeem Phillip
YASH	Praneet Akilla
YEBI	Kai Bradbury
DONNA/BOY	Yoshié Bancroft
CHARLIE	Andrea Menard
PAUL	Tom McBeath

Directed by Jovanni Sy
Set Design: Marshall McMahen
Costume Design: Barbara Clayden
Lighting Design: Sophie Tang
Sound Design: Joelysa Pankanea
Stage Manager: Angela Beaulieu
Assistant Director and
Cultural Consultant: Gavan Cheema

Foreword

Sarena Parmar has achieved something quite surprising with her *Orchard*. Cleaving very closely to the source text, following it moment-to-moment at times, but transplanting it into a new context, she has transformed a work about the fading Russian aristocracy of the late 19th century into a play about postcolonial Canada, a *brown Cherry Orchard*.

As in Chekhov's play, and like the mortgage melodramas Chekhov modelled his play on, at the centre of the drama is a property which will be auctioned off if its owners cannot find the money to pay their debts. As in the Chekhov, the (Basran) family rejects a proposal that might save their property but transform it, because of their love of the place as it is. However, in Parmar's version this love for the property is a product of their labour, not simply a sentimental attachment.

> Well I can smell the dirt. And not just any dirt, this is Morning Dirt. Smells musty, like clay. And when I walk back to the house for dinner every day, the last thing I smell is the Sunset Dirt. Smells like an earthworm that's been baking in the sun with his swim trunks all day. But my favourite is the midday heat, it's dry and hot. And the dirt smells like the fuzz of a peach.

The speaker is Gurjit (or Gus) Basran, one of the three generations of Sikh farmers that own the orchard. The remarkable olfactory acuity he reveals here is both a signal and a product of his intense affiliation with this particular place. He is so intimately connected to the land that he can parse different qualities of the soil, interrelating them in a description that speaks to his deeply embodied relationship to the orchard. He is, after all, "a farmer… Like my father and his father before him" and his "heart gets weary if [he's] not up at the crack of dawn." Kesur, his father, explains that the family hails from Punjab, which "means land of the five rivers, so green you can grow anything. Back and back and back, we have been farmers since the birth of those five rivers. That is in the blood." Of course, farming is not literally "in the blood." What Kesur essentializes here is the sense of deeply belonging, of connection to a particular place produced by farming. The self-definition produced by that labour feels internal, essential, like lifeblood.

Loveleen, Gurjit's sister recently returned from Bombay, expresses her attachment to this particular place too. "God, I love this country, I had forgotten, my own country! It made me weep on the bus. I pressed my cheek against the window and I felt the cool mountain air on the glass, and it made me cry even more." Though she often, like Ranyevskaya in the source text, relates her emotions upon her return to her childhood – "Oh god, my childhood. So pure" – these childhood memories are also related to work on the farm. "I woke up every morning to the same sound. Mummy whistling and starting the sprinklers." Theirs is a fully embodied relationship to the orchard.

While work on the farm produces a deeply embodied sense of belonging, of rootedness, of "home," there are social and political developments that could acknowledge, magnify, and legitimize these feelings. Set in the 1970s, the play deftly explores the promise and challenges of the multicultural ideal when it was first introduced. While some (like Annie, a Chekhovian idealist willing to work to see the future come to pass) are optimistic about the possibilities, others (like the white neighbour, Paul) feel that any change will have to be managed "responsibly," by which he probably means that a racial status quo must not be upset. The quiet(ly Canadian) racial tensions that exist in the play burst into the open in the 'mendicant scene' in Act 2, and are more thoroughly explored in Barminder's moving storyline.

The effort, the labour that each of the brown characters puts in in order to make a place here – each struggles to belong – is carefully observed by the playwright/adaptor. Parmar further complicates the issue of belonging with Charlie, a First Nations former rodeo queen, who also works on the farm. Like Charlotta in the source text, Charlie sometimes entertains the guests and family, though she performs rodeo rather than card tricks.

More importantly, she represents another claim on the land at the heart of the play. A residential school survivor, Charlie has at best patchy access to her roots or family. Where the Basrans can claim a heritage as old as the five rivers of Punjab, Charlie has only scattered memories of things her grandfather taught her. She has "no parents, no story […] I don't even have a birth certificate, so I still act young." However, Charlie is not defeated or crushed by her position or lack of family connections. "I'm a lost generation," she says but then appends the phrase, "so they say." Elsewhere, Charlie says, "Who am I? No one can tell me…," which might sound like a lament, but we also understand it includes the possibility of forging her own identity and relationship to her world.

Transplanting Chekhov to the Okanagan Valley, Parmar interrogates the thorny questions of ownership, attachment and belonging that still underscore much political and theoretical debate in Canada. She has brought a degree of complexity to this inquiry of which Chekhov might approve; perhaps more surprisingly, she has brought the kind of emotional generosity to her characters that Chekhov himself practised. As with Chekhov, it is we, her readers and audiences, who are the real beneficiaries.

Guillermo Verdecchia
Head of Play Development, Soulpepper Theatre

Production Notes

Notes on the Text

All characters have Canadian accents. Except for Kesur who has a Punjabi accent, and Barbra who might have a slight Punjabi cadence to her speech.

Often characters speak in non-sequiturs, especially in group scenes. Although they are listening to the conversation on some level, they are wrapped up in their own fears, passions, and longings.

/   The next speaker should overlap their dialogue at the slash.

—   The speaker's thought is interrupted, either by themselves, or the next speaker.

…   The speaker gets lost or suspended in a thought.

Text in bolded open brackets ( ) indicates English translation of Punjabi, Gurbani or Japanese phrases.

Publisher's Note: Inconsistencies in grammar and punctuation throughout the text appear at the express request of the author, and are intended to aid in the flow of the spoken text.

For example, sometimes commas are used for direct address, other times they are omitted. Sometimes nouns are capitalized for emphasis, other times proper nouns are not capitalized to indicate that they should carry no added emphasis.

Orchard Interludes

The interludes are the memories conjured by the Orchard.

The voice-overs should sound intimate. The images are poetic.

A Note on the World

Like many immigrants of that time, the non-white characters believe they are guests in this country. The only exception is Charlie.

Characters

LOVELEEN is around 50.
Charismatic. But cannot face the death of her husband and son. She has made life a distraction to avoid the grief.

Nicknames Lallie and Lovely. South Asian. Shares land ownership with her brother.

GURJIT is in his late 40s.
Young at heart. He loves to solve problems with his imagination. He faces more racism than he admits to himself.

Nickname Gus. South Asian. Younger brother of LOVELEEN.

ANNIE is in her 20s.
Darling and mediator of the family. A passionate idealist. She is a girl on the precipice of her womanhood.

South Asian. Daughter of LOVELEEN.

BARBRA is in her late 20s.
Exhausted. She manages the majority of the household. Her pursuit to assimilate costs Barbra her soul.

Given name Barminder. South Asian. Niece of LOVELEEN and GURJIT.

KESUR is around 80.
Grounded. It's like he is a part of the land. The moral centre of the family. He is acutely observant. All his stories are roundabout ways to give them the guidance they need.

South Asian. Father of LOVELEEN and GURJIT.

MICHAEL LOPAKHIN is in his 30s.
An awkward sense of humour. Good-hearted. He loves the Basran family deeply. Michael's Achilles heel is his own ambition.

Caucasian. Self-made businessman.

PETER is in his late 20s.
Passionate and intelligent. He was the last person to see Griesha alive, and carries the weight of that responsibility.

South Asian. Family friend of the Basrans.

YASH is in his late 20s.
A ladies man. Behind his bravado, he is fiercely loyal to the Basrans. In his eyes, they raised him.

South Asian. Grew up around the Basran home, like extended family.

YEBI is around 30.
Despite his troubles, he always has a happy-go-lucky attitude. His name literally means Shrimp Mountain. His admiration of cowboys is true and real.

Given name, Yebisaka. Japanese. Handyman and fruit picker for the Basrans.

DONNA is around 25.
Flighty. She loves the feeling of being in love. She aspires to be sophisticated which she also associates with being Caucasian.

Given name, Sanae. Japanese. Works for the Basrans in the fruit stand.

CHARLIE is in her 60s.
Unsentimental. She is comfortable being a lone wolf. She shares a special kinship with Kesur, and fondness for the family.

First Nations. Fruit picker for the Basrans.

PAUL is around 50.
A big-hearted and robust personality. Salt-of-the-earth farmer. Unaware of his racial biases.

Caucasian. Owns the orchard next to the Basrans.

GRIESHA was six.
Drowned six years ago in the creek. He was the hope of the family to keep the orchard running for the generation to come.

South Asian. Youngest child of LOVELEEN.

BOY is about 13.
The age Griesha would have been if he were still alive. Entitled but poor.

Caucasian.

THE ORCHARD
(*After Chekhov*)

Land Acknowledgement.[1]

Before the show. House lights up. The actor playing CHARLIE and the actor playing ANNIE enter in Canadian dress from the 1970s.

They address the audience as themselves; it has an informal feel. The actor playing ANNIE asks the audience to please turn off their cell phones. The actor playing CHARLIE might start the Land Acknowledgement by saying "Welcome" in whichever Indigenous languages are appropriate. The actors talk about our shared responsibility of caring for the land. The actor playing CHARLIE acknowledges the traditional peoples on whose land the play is being performed. The actor playing ANNIE acknowledges the Syilx People and their unceded lands of the Okanagan, where the story takes place. The greeting concludes with the actor playing Annie saying, "Welcome to The Orchard (After Chekhov)!"

---

1   A description from the original production. Because the land acknowledgement is a living, breathing relationship with the audience, we decided not to write the verbatim dialogue, but rather a description of the event, as it is integral to the show but changes with each production.

Because this play is about land and who has "ownership" of that land, it is important to the playwright that a land acknowledgment begins every show. It should always be researched in consultation with Indigenous Elders, and acknowledge the region in which the play is performed, as well as where the play is set.

As the conversation around land acknowledgements continues to evolve, each production should re-examine this section, led by the Indigenous actor playing Charlie in dialogue with the playwright.

Orchard Interlude. Springtime.

The stage is dark.

GRIESHA v.o.
(Whispers.) Springtime.

The Basran Orchard, Spring 1969.

Sounds of birds singing, perhaps one flutters away. Early morning. Nature sounds in the orchard.

The voice-over is distorted, far away in time.

GRIESHA v.o.
(Examining a tree.)
Mom! A blossom! A blossom!

A warm shaft of light streams onstage. The sun rises on a small house made from children's building blocks.

~~~~

KESUR v.o.
Griesha has a way with the orchard. He understands it. Just like you, Lovely.

~~~~

LOVELEEN v.o.
(Working side-by-side with her father.)
Do you think these old trees will make it?

KESUR v.o.
I've been farming for sixty years, and one thing I know for sure: you can't tell a tree what to do, they're stubborn as hell.

The birds sing a little longer.

CHARLIE enters. She moves the toy house.

It remains somewhere onstage throughout the play.

Act One. Scene One.

The Okanagan Valley. The Basran Living Room. Late April, 1974. Early morning.

"A New World in the Morning" by Roger Whittaker is playing on the radio.

MICHAEL is asleep. BARBRA enters, tired from a bad night's sleep, from months and years of hard work that is never enough. She goes into the other room.

RADIO ANNOUNCER: News for the valley on Friday, April 25th, 1974. The spring regatta was a roaring success, with thousands of people descending on our beautiful valley. It was four days of sun, water and fireworks. And then there was this young man, who was on a serious hunt, for none other than the Ogopogo.

Meanwhile the phone rings in the other room, DONNA runs to pick it up. BARBRA comes back with chaa.[2] She listens to the radio intently, checking the time and looking out the window.

LOCAL LITTLE BOY: (*Singing a-cappella, like a nursery rhyme.*)
I'm looking for the Ogopogo,
The funny little Ogopogo.
His mother was an earwig,
his father was a whale,
I'm going to put a little bit of salt
on his tail.[3]

---

2   Tea in Punjabi, made with milk and Indian spices.
3   *The Ogo-Pogo: The Funny Fox-Trot*, composed by Cumberland Clark.

> RADIO ANNOUNCER: In other news, it's been two years since Minister of Agriculture David Stupich pushed his Land Freeze Bill through the NDP majority house.
>
> *BARBRA turns up the radio.*
>
> Farmers continue to kick back against the Land Freeze, as profits from family farms continue to decline year after year, with many farms falling into bankruptcy –
>
> *BARBRA turns off the radio.*

DONNA: Politics are so boring!

BARBRA: (*Startled.*) Donna! Jesus! Are you still up?

DONNA: Are you kidding?!

BARBRA: Yes, the big homecoming…

DONNA: Nothing to worry about after tonight. Not even this stupid frost.

BARBRA: Damn it, there's frost again?! God help us.

> *BARBRA starts putting on her boots, looking out the window.*

Can you tell Yebi to get the tractor ready.

> *BARBRA rushes out. The door slams behind her. MICHAEL wakes with a start.*

MICHAEL: Welcome home Lallie! (*Realizing no one is there.*) Oh. What time is it?

DONNA: Nearly 5 a.m.

MICHAEL: My gawd.

DONNA: Gus called, they just got in.

MICHAEL: (*Yawning.*) That makes the Greyhound... (*Checking watch.*) Three hours late.

DONNA: I thought you'd left with everybody else. But then I found you here, sleeping like a bear.

MICHAEL: Why didn't you wake me?

DONNA: Oh.

MICHAEL: I came early to greet them from the station. Ah, look, my suit's all wrinkled.

DONNA: (*Listening.*) Is that the truck?

MICHAEL: Donna, it'll take at least fifteen minutes to get from the station, plus unloading and all that. *Five* years. I wonder what Lallie looks like?

DONNA: Miss Basran was always so beautiful. The pickers loved her.

MICHAEL: 'Cause she got right in there with them. Working side by side! I remember when I first met her. My old man, he used to have this trailer, out on that Indian land. This one time, I forgot to turn the sprinkler off. Well my old man got real angry with me. He took that hose and whipped me straight across the head. My ear was bleeding like crazy. Anyway, I took myself into town – you know, to lift my spirits. I must have been about twelve standing there, a hot mess, blood coming outta my ear, and that's when I saw her. Lallie. She bent down, sun glowing behind her, and said, don't worry little man, one day you'll be older, and you'll be free. (*Beat.*) Never called me trash like the rest of them.

DONNA: Sorry, what were you saying? Oh, look, my hands are shaking. I think I'm going to faint.

MICHAEL: You're too delicate, Donna.

DONNA: (*Bragging.*) The doctor says I'm hypoglycaemic.

MICHAEL: That's what I mean. Your hair is always in some extravagant sculpture. You should try and fit in with your common man.

DONNA: I saw another foreclosure letter stuffed in the bookcase.

MICHAEL: (*Absorbed in his own problem.*) Do you think I should say my condolences or something? About the boy. I didn't see her after the funeral.

DONNA: No one saw her after the funeral. She got straight on a plane and never looked back. (*Sighing.*) What an adventure… The dogs have been barking like crazy. It's like they *sense* Miss Basran is coming home.

> *YEBI enters with a bunch of wild flowers. He wears a new pair of cowboy boots. They are uncomfortable and squeak loudly.*

YEBI: Good morning my heart–s. (*Giving DONNA the flowers.*) Donna, these are from the groundskeeper.

DONNA: Freddie? But we fired him three months ago.

YEBI: (*Caught, but he soldiers on.*) And he said, to water them – twice – a – day.

> *DONNA goes to the kitchen with the flowers.*

MICHAEL: Donna, I need some coffee.

DONNA: We have chaa.

MICHAEL: Fine, that's fine.

> *DONNA exits.*

YEBI: This weather! Dipped again last night. If the frost doesn't let up, that'll be it for the blossoms. No blossoms, no harvest, no money. Ah! The power of nature!

MICHAEL: Yes! Lallie can't get here soon enough. Lots of business to discuss tonight.

YEBI: My friend, do you mind if I ask you something in confidence? You see, I bought these boots, authentic cowboy boots, from Mr. Glenmore, brand new. But the problem is they squeak. Just look…

YEBI demonstrates. The boots squeak. He sighs.

I don't know what to do. Do you know, is there a balm or an oil…? I'm afraid the squeak won't leave naturally. You know, with general use.

MICHAEL: Yebi. There is *nothing* that can help you.

YEBI: Every day one thing or another happens to me. An unpleasant kind of thing. But I don't complain. I've even gotten used to it. Look, I can even laugh at it.

DONNA enters with chaa for MICHAEL.

BARBRA: (*Offstage.*) (*Angry.*) Yebi! Where are you?!

YEBI: I'll be going then Donna.

YEBI bumps into a table, things fall over. He tries to clean it up in vain. Everything falls again.

Ah ha! You see! (*Triumphantly.*) This is it, so to speak! It's simply extraordinary. Situations that baffle the mind…

YEBI goes out.

DONNA: Michael I have to tell you something. Oh no, I can't. Only if I don't tell somebody I may burst. Or die! It's not healthy to keep a secret. But it's not ladylike to say.

MICHAEL: Out with it, Donna.

DONNA: Yebi proposed to me!

MICHAEL: Again?

DONNA: At the regatta fireworks. It was so romantic. All the colours flashing over the mountains. And Yebi was there too, of course. He's a lovely sort of man, don't you think? He seems sensitive. Only... I can't understand anything he says.

MICHAEL: Shh! Hear that? *Yeess* they're here! I'm going to meet them at the truck. I wonder if she'll recognize me? Forgot my mints. Five years.

MICHAEL exits.

DONNA: Oh I'm going to faint. I *am* fainting.

Car doors slam outside. People greet each other in a mix of Punjabi and English. LOVELEEN, ANNIE, BARBRA, and GURJIT enter. LOVELEEN is wearing an extravagant sari. ANNIE wears a salwaar kameez. GURJIT is turbaned and bearded.

Everyone watches LOVELEEN with excitement and uneasiness. She has not stepped foot in the house since GRIESHA's funeral. Unsure of her emotional state, they handle her delicately.

ANNIE: Mom, hurry! Look, my room. I still have the blanket you made me.

LOVELEEN: Oh your room! This window, those curtains!

BARBRA: It's freezing out there.

LOVELEEN: And the nursery... It's locked?

BARBRA: We use it for storage now.

ANNIE: (*Discreetly.*) Barbra do we?

BARBRA shakes her head "no."

LOVELEEN: Donna, what are you doing here in the middle of the night?

DONNA: (*Blurting.*) I like your outfit!!

ANNIE: She lives here now.

BARBRA: Room and board.

LOVELEEN: (*With a melancholy happiness.*) This chair... I used to sit right here and watch our fruit stand. Yes, when I was a little girl. So many hours in *this* raggedy chair.

> *KESUR enters with work boots and tools; he is turbaned and bearded. LOVELEEN sees him for the first time since arriving home.*
>
> *Pause.*

Papa... is that you?

KESUR: We have all been missing you, Lovely.

LOVELEEN: It's been a while...

> *LOVELEEN and KESUR share a look, but she is unable to go to him. Beat.*
>
> *LOVELEEN changes the mood, effortlessly and with charm, in that way only she could.*

Ah, what was I saying?! And tonight, I am that girl again! Donna Naito, you've turned into a woman! And Barbra! Why do you look like a nun?

BARBRA: I'll put some wood in the stove.

> *MICHAEL, YASH, PAUL, and CHARLIE enter from outside.*

YASH: You know, the bus was three hours late! Ha, how's that for Western efficiency. Lovely, we should have stayed in India.

> *ANNIE exits.*

PAUL: (*To the Basrans.*) Hello! I saw the light on, I thought I'd stop by.

MICHAEL: Lallie, can I just say you look extraordinary.

PAUL: (*To CHARLIE.*) Apples. That's where the money is.

CHARLIE: My horse is apple intolerant.

PAUL: It... really?

Everyone goes out joking.

Inside ANNIE and BARBRA's bedroom.

ANNIE: Oh god, my room, I've missed you. Hello sweet Teddy. (*To TEDDY.*) Tomorrow as soon as we get up, I'm going to run through the orchard!

BARBRA enters unnoticed.

BARBRA: Our darling girl is home again.

ANNIE: Where did I put my hair elastic...?

BARBRA: (*Dangling ANNIE's jeans.*) Forget about these?

ANNIE: Oh my god, my jeans! I'm never taking these off again!

They hug.

BARBRA: You were supposed to be home six weeks ago.

BOTH: I missed you.

ANNIE: (*Beat.*) So... mom looks *different*...

BARBRA: Was she dressed like that the entire time? She looks like she's about to get married!!

ANNIE: Lay off, Barbra. I brought her back, didn't I?

BARBRA: Oh God, Annie! Who the hell is that?!

ANNIE: It's mom! She's just –

BARBRA: You can't farm in a silk sari!

ANNIE: Stop yelling at me.

BARBRA: We spent the last of our savings on your plane tickets. What happened over there?

ANNIE: If you must know, Bombay was awful. She wasn't at dad's apartment on Nariman Point –

BARBRA: Annie! What are you saying? Why / didn't you call?!

ANNIE: Relax Barbra. This thing is so itchy!

> *She tears off her salwaar kameez, and puts on jeans and a t-shirt.*

When I find her? You won't believe it Barbra – she's renting this dirty room above a fish shop. The windows are boarded up, the place is full of smoke. It's suffocating. But there's mom, sitting in the corner, looking like the Queen of Bombay. (*Beat.*) I thought she liked our farm clothes.

And Yash is there too – acting like mom's driver – but she's too broke for a car – he's egging her on to stay! And her friends!? They're parasites. Throwing parties and passing out on the floor. It was sick. And do you hear the way she laughs now? …Then one day, that man sends a letter.

> *They share a beat.*

Mom just… she held my face so tight and… (*ANNIE stops herself.*) She said, "Let's go *home*." And we got on a plane the next day.

BARBRA: She's the only one who understands the orchard, and now look at her.

ANNIE: I'm making it sound bad. Watch, she'll be wearing that ugly flannel thing and working on the tractor before you know it. This plan will work Barbra. (*Beat.*) And guess what?! In Bombay, I saw all these cool temples and I met a baby monkey!

BARBRA: (*Softening.*) Oh Annie.

ANNIE: What about here? Did the bank defer our payments?

BARBRA: Far from it. It's official. If we don't pay, the property will go up for auction.

ANNIE: Oh god.

BARBRA: We'd lose everything. The house, the orchard...

ANNIE: Oh god.

BARBRA: The fact is: we need a perfect harvest, and even then...

> *MICHAEL sneaks into the room. He doesn't see the girls and starts airing out the sweat stains on his shirt.*

ANNIE: Hi Michael.

> *MICHAEL jumps back seeing ANNIE and BARBRA.*

MICHAEL: Ah, these wrinkles. (*Bleating like a goat.*) Meeeeh! What was that?

BARBRA: Ooh shoo!

> *MICHAEL exits. Beat.*

ANNIE: (*In a hushed tone.*) Barbra, has he proposed yet?

> *BARBRA indicates "no."*

Why not? Michael loves you. I can feel it.

BARBRA: I see him at church all the time. Susan doesn't think we're a good match. Maybe she's right, there's no ring. Nothing. It all feels like a cruel joke.

ANNIE: Since when are you hanging out at the church?

BARBRA: Everyone hangs out there. It's like eating meat.

ANNIE: But you don't eat meat. Oh my god, do you?!

BARBRA: No! Anyway the church has been very nice to us. Look, the girls gave me this bible as a kind of welcome present to the group. Here, hold it.

ANNIE: (*Unsure.*) It's beautiful.

BARBRA: It's more or less the same teachings: be good, don't steal, help others.

BARBRA holds the bible with ANNIE.

BARBRA: This passage is my favourite. "The Lord is my shepherd; I shall not want. He makes me lie down in green pastures; He leads me to still waters. He restores my soul."[4]

ANNIE: I don't think you should keep this in here.

Outside ANNIE and BARBRA's bedroom. KESUR enters with DONNA.

KESUR: Oye girl! How long does it take to make chaa? This is looking like watered milk!

DONNA: Oh god, I forgot the tea bag again!

KESUR: That girl can't tell pickles from peaches.

KESUR starts laughing to himself. His laughter becomes bigger and bigger.

BARBRA: (*Yelling from the bedroom.*) (*In Punjabi.*) ਵੱਡੇ ਬਾਬਾ ਜੀ, ਤੁਸੀ ਕਿਉਂ ਦੰਦ ਕੱਢੀ ਜਾਨੇ ਆਂ? **(Big grandpa, what are you laughing at?)**

KESUR: (*In Punjabi.*) ਕੀ ਬੇਟੀ? **(What bhitee[5]?)**

ANNIE: What's so funny?

---

4   Psalm 23:1-3
5   Little darling in Punjabi.

KESUR: Sell it all! It doesn't matter. The family is together again. And now I can die.

In the living room. LOVELEEN, GURJIT, MICHAEL, YASH, and PAUL have been socializing. ANNIE, KESUR, and DONNA enter. BARBRA follows.

GURJIT: Once upon a time we played pirates in this very room. Do you remember Lovely?

LOVELEEN: Oh yes! And how does it go? Wendy walks the plank.

GURJIT: And Peter Pan to the rescue! Little children. And now we're older and this room is still here. Thirty-eight years ago. How strange.

MICHAEL: Time flies!

GURJIT: What?

MICHAEL: I said time flies.

GURJIT: It still smells like the open sea…

BARBRA: (*To LOVELEEN and company.*) All right friends, time to pack it in.

Everyone groans in protest.

LOVELEEN: Ohhh, Barminder. You're exactly the same, so serious. Let us have our drinks and we promise to be quiet. Please…? In Bombay, they drink tea day and night. I've gotten used to it. It doesn't even keep me up. (*KESUR passes her tea.*) Thank you-ji.

YASH: (*To KESUR.*) I'll have some chaa too. One sugar, thank you.

PAUL: Tell us more about India. Did you eat goat?

LOVELEEN: I ate shark!

PAUL: Imagine that! How exotic!

> *BARBRA retrieves a letter from a locked cabinet.*

BARBRA: A letter from India, mussi-ji.[6]

LOVELEEN: I'm finished with that place.

> *LOVELEEN refuses the letter. There is an awkward silence.*

PAUL: Well another one of those government boys stopped by my property last week.

MICHAEL: Are they still trying to rezone the land?

GURJIT: They *captured* us last year, I'm afraid.

PAUL: But who's growing on that land? Not them in their fancy offices with their business lunches.

LOVELEEN: Are you still picking on their lunches?!

PAUL: It's me. With these hands and this aching back. Besides, if I grow a potato for 15 cents and can only sell it for 12 cents –

> *MICHAEL tries to join in, but doesn't know the punch line and mumbles along.*

LOVELEEN/GURJIT: I should just eat the potato myself!

MICHAEL: Myself!!

> *There is an awkward silence.*

> *Outside, CHARLIE enters and starts fixing farm equipment. She works unobserved.*

Well. I should be going. I've got business up north, big meeting in Prince George tomorrow, very important. I just wanted to stop by and… it's a shame we didn't get to – well you look radiant, just glowing… ah, I really wanted to stay/and talk to you about…

---

6 Aunt in Punjabi. Specifically, the sister of one's mother.

PAUL: /yes back from your adventures and dressed in the latest...

PAUL is unable to describe LOVELEEN's Indian outfit.

MICHAEL: Lallie, your brother has never liked me. We can joke about it because it's true. I only hope that... You showed me a kindness once, a mercy that I will never forget... And somehow I made something of myself, and my only wish is to repay that debt to you because, I've come to think of you as a friend, as more than a friend even –

LOVELEEN jumps up and walks about the room in great agitation.

LOVELEEN: Oh dear! I... I have to take in this room!

ANNIE: Yes!

LOVELEEN: What is this happiness overtaking me? *This* room. Do you remember when I took this picture Gurjit? I loved that camera.

GURJIT: And then Barbra became the family "photographhière." You know James Mackey from next door died.

PAUL: His son took over the orchard.

LOVELEEN: (*Sits down to drink tea.*) I didn't know that.

GURJIT: And Miss Linda passed too.

LOVELEEN: So much death! This place is like a funeral home. We should start charging for tickets.

Everyone shares an uncomfortable look, except LOVELEEN.

MICHAEL: I want to say something jolly! (*Looks at watch.*) Ah, I should get going. There's never enough time to say these things properly. So, I'm just gonna come out and say it: as you know, on the 22nd of August this orchard goes up for auction.

LOVELEEN: I'm sorry, what…? Auction?

GURJIT: Annie didn't tell you?

An uncomfortable beat.

MICHAEL: But…! What I've come to say is this: You can save the property! And even make additional money. Yes, it's a miracle!

Now since the property is in the land freeze, it must be used for agriculture. But you can use *part* of the land for other purposes.

LOVELEEN: Gus, I'm sure I don't understand him.

MICHAEL: If I may… An *Agricultural RV Park!*

Outside. CHARLIE exits.

ANNIE: /What!?

GURJIT: This is/ridiculous!

PAUL: Gimme a break!

MICHAEL: All the amenities of an RV site with the charm of nature!

Everyone laughs or groans at MICHAEL's proposal, except BARBRA and LOVELEEN.

Maybe even a restaurant one day. City hall can't complain. And if you advertise now, I'd stake my reputation that you'll be full up with customers before the first fruit harvest. The plots will get snatched up like that! Of course you'd have to cut down most of the orchard. Everything that doesn't legally need to be in the land freeze.

ANNIE: Cut? I'm sorry, what are you/saying –

GURJIT: Cut!?

MICHAEL: Tourists flock here like crazy in the summer. We're close to all the beaches and hiking, excetera. We're a haven! You get a contractor to run a sewage line, hydro hookup and a paved spot for each RV… Charge a fee, say $100 a week per pad, with 25 campers during a four-month summer, that's $40,000! And all I have to say to that is congratulations! Yes congratulations, because you're saved! Now, I think the cherry trees should be cut first. They take the most amount of coddling anyway. And the house, it's served a good turn, yes? Demo it as well, and you could get five extra plots.

GURJIT: Do you know this is the best soil in the entire valley to grow cherries? The perfect amount of sunlight, the mountains keep the rain off. We're in the encyclopedia.

MICHAEL: The only exceptional thing about this orchard is that it's old and large.

GURJIT: SunRype has expressed interest.

MICHAEL: You only produce a viable crop every other year. The orchard and *everything* on it will be repossessed in August. I can see I've hit an emotional spot, but please see things clearly.

GURJIT: Tell me Mr. Lopakhin, when you walk up to the house, what do you smell?

MICHAEL: Fresh air. No, actually just tractor grease.

GURJIT: Well I can smell the dirt. And not just any dirt, this is Morning Dirt. Smells musty, like clay. And when I walk back to the house for dinner every day, the last thing I smell is the Sunset Dirt. Smells like an earthworm that's been baking in the sun with his swim trunks all day. But my favourite is the midday heat, it's dry and hot. And the dirt smells like the fuzz of a peach.

We are farmers, my friend. Like my father and his father before him. Not some businessman. May not be glamorous work to someone like you, but my heart gets weary if I'm not up at the crack of dawn.

KESUR: (*Slowly.*) Your mother would hang bells in those cherry trees. She brought those silver bells from your grandmother's mango field in India. And before mango, it was cotton. We come from Punjab, land of the five rivers, so green you can grow anything. Back and back and back, we have been farmers since the birth of those five rivers. That is in the blood. (*Laughing.*) Your mother said the silver bells kept the birds away.

LOVELEEN: And did it?

KESUR: Who knows. Ask the birds.

YASH: Lovely, it's time for your pills.[7]

PAUL: Oh no, Lallie! *Don't* take those awful things. (*Taking the pills.*) I confiscate them!

LOVELEEN: Are you mad?

> *PAUL shakes the pills onto his hand, blows on them and then suddenly passes out. The pills scatter.*

---

[7] Quaaludes, or an anti-anxiety medication. Loveleen was prescribed the pills after Griesha's death.

YASH: He's asleep!

Everyone laughs.

MICHAEL: Like a bird against a window!

Everyone stops laughing.

I would like to say one more thing. One thing. Thirty years ago, what did we have? There were professionals and there were workers. And now what do we have? A third type of lifestyle. Vacationers, vacation seekers, tourism! The baby boomers retire and this market will explode. Sure, at first they might only stay for the summer. But in time, they'll grow attached, start skiing in the winters. You'll have people year round, filling the orchard with life and laughter and profit once again!!

Silence.

The family looks to LOVELEEN. Beat.

LOVELEEN: These silly pills. They're everywhere.

YASH: Allow me, Lovely. Really, it's no problem.

YASH picks up the pills.

MICHAEL: Truly, Lallie, it's the only way. Promise me you'll sleep on it. (*Glancing at watch.*) I gotta get going...

CHARLIE enters.

Charlie, our lone wanderer! And where did you disappear to? I haven't said a proper hello.

MICHAEL goes to kiss CHARLIE's hand.

CHARLIE: First the hand, then the elbow... I know these games. What do you wanna kiss next?

MICHAEL: No luck… no luck at all today. Miss Charlie, how about one of your rodeo tricks?

CHARLIE: I don't think so.

CHARLIE exits.

MICHAEL: Ah, I really wish I could stay longer, but when the sun comes up I turn into a pumpkin. (*Kissing LOVELEEN's hand.*) Goodbye Lallie. I'll see you in three weeks' time. Sir, thank you for –

GURJIT: Goodbye.

MICHAEL: That's it then. Goodbye Barbra. (*Waking PAUL.*) Paul, Paul, Paul, I'm leaving. (*To LOVELEEN.*) If you change your mind about the RV park, it's really no trouble to get you the financing… Yash, good to see you. See you later, old man!

BARBRA: Will you please go away. Please.

MICHAEL: Yes, yes of course. Buenos dwee-ohs, mes amis!

MICHAEL exits.

GURJIT: That man is insufferable!

ANNIE and PAUL stifle a laugh.

(*Playfully.*) Oh oh dear, now I've done it. Barminder, our bride to be, I beg your pardon, speaking of your fiancé like that.

BARBRA: It's fine, mama-ji,[8] just leave it.

PAUL: Well congratulations, my dear! My Brenda says he's quite the catch. Ah, let's just say it, he's a handsome guy!

GURJIT, ANNIE, and PAUL chuckle lightly. The laughter subsides. Long beat.

---

8   Uncle in Punjabi. Specifically, the brother of one's mother.

LOVELEEN: (*To Gus.*) ...Foreclosure?

GURJIT: Yes.

LOVELEEN: The house? The orchard?

> *Uncomfortable beat.*

PAUL: A run of bad luck, that's all.

> *Uncomfortable beat.*

GURJIT: Sister, do you know how old this bookcase is?

LOVELEEN: No.

GURJIT: The other day I pulled a drawer out, and do you know what I found? A date stamped on the bottom from the manufacturer.

> *YASH passes LOVELEEN a pill and a glass of water.*

LOVELEEN: Thank you, Yash.

GURJIT: This bookcase has accomplished one hundred years of life. Imagine that. A centennial. If a person were a hundred years old we would throw a parade. But no, not for a bookcase, an inanimate object.

PAUL: One hundred years. Well that's something.

GURJIT: Yes. A valuable piece of history... Bookcase: I salute you!! You have held knowledge in the highest regard for one hundred years. Lifted our ideals to their zenith, educated us... kept ideas safe behind your walls... you have guarded the gates well, my friend.

LOVELEEN: Gus-phaajee,[9] you haven't changed a bit.

GURJIT: (*Embarrassed.*) Just, just walk the plank.

---

9   Brother in Punjabi.

ANNIE: Mom, I'm going to bed.

LOVELEEN: My one and only. Are you happy to be home?

ANNIE: Yes. With you back, it feels like a dream.

GURJIT: You look just like your mother. Doesn't she, Lovely? Just like you at that age.

> *PAUL gets up to say goodnight to ANNIE, but she leaves.*

LOVELEEN: Excuse her. She's so tired.

PAUL: I can only imagine. A journey like that. It's clear on the other side of the world!

LOVELEEN: Well, I've finished my tea.

YASH: (*Laughing.*) Lovely, do you remember smoking hookah in Bombay –

LOVELEEN: In that terrible bar next to the train yard!

GURJIT: You should probably get the luggage, Yash.

YASH: Fine. I can drink this later.

> *YASH exits.*

LOVELEEN: And now what will we do? Dance!

> *Everyone cheers!*

> *Inside ANNIE and BARBRA's bedroom.*

DONNA: You'll never guess who arrived the day before yesterday.

ANNIE: Who?

DONNA: Prabhas Thiara.

ANNIE: Peter?!

DONNA: He's been sleeping in the pickers' cabins. "I don't want to be an inconvenience," he said. But the truth is Barbra stuck him there. She doesn't want Miss Basran to see him until tomorrow.

BARBRA enters unnoticed.

ANNIE: I thought he was studying abroad.

DONNA: He was doing a term in India, but he dropped out/ of that –

BARBRA: Donna, could you make some more chaa. (*To ANNIE.*) None for you cousin. (*To DONNA.*) And put out some snack mix[10] and badaam.[11]

DONNA: Yes of course. (*To ANNIE.*) He started working with all these politicians.

ANNIE: Why did he come back?

DONNA: He says he ran out of money, but –

BARBRA: Donna. That's enough.

DONNA: Sorry.

BARBRA: Wait! Don't put out the spicy mix, Paul is staying.

DONNA exits.

Outside ANNIE and BARBRA's bedroom. YASH enters, carrying more luggage.

YASH: Hey, my old hat.

YASH puts on his cowboy hat.

DONNA: Yash, is that you? I barely recognized you. You've changed abroad.

YASH: Sorry, who are you?

---

10   Chevda in Punjabi. An Indian snack mix made of fried chickpea flour, lentils and spices.
11   Nuts in Punjabi..

DONNA: When you left I was still in high school... across the bridge. I'm Donna, Joe Naito's niece. He owns the orchard up the road? (*Takes YASH's cowboy hat.*) You really don't remember me?

YASH: Do you know what happens when you take a cowboy's hat?

DONNA: No.

YASH: It means you're going home with him.

> *YASH pinches DONNA. She squeals and drops a plate. YASH takes his hat.*

BARBRA: What's going on out here?

DONNA: I broke a plate.

BARBRA: Well that's good luck.

ANNIE: We should warn mom that Peter's here.

BARBRA: Oh, now you want to tell mussi-ji everything. You had six weeks Annie! She didn't know anything, about the bank, the debts, the foreclosure!

ANNIE: I didn't want to scare her away. You see, I'm the only one that understands her.

BARBRA: Fine. Then she can see Peter tomorrow, or next week. Or never, if it were up to me.

ANNIE: She's all right now. It's been five years since Griesha drowned.

BARBRA: Right after your dad died. And then mussi-ji left us.

ANNIE: And now she's home. Just give her a chance, Barbra.

BARBRA: No, it's too much.

In the living room, country music is playing. Everyone is enjoying the mood, perhaps singing along. BARBRA enters and turns the music off. People groan.

LOVELEEN: Am I really sitting here? I feel like jumping on all the furniture! (*Hiding her face in her hands.*) What if this is just a dream? No. Because here we all are! Drinking *this* tea. That *you* gave me, papa-ji.[12] I'm glad you're still alive.

KESUR: The day before yesterday.

GURJIT: He refuses to put in his hearing aid. (*To KESUR.*) We're glad you're still with us baba-ji.[13]

KESUR: (*In Punjabi.*) ਉ ਕੀ ਕਿਹਾ? **(What?)**

GURJIT: I said, the family…. We're happy you're not dead!

BARBRA goes downstage. She looks through a window, taking in the orchard, as if she can breathe it in through the glass.

BARBRA: It feels warmer today. Look mussi-ji, you're just in time for the bloom.

LOVELEEN joins BARBRA at the window. She stares at their beautiful orchard for the first time since her arrival.

LOVELEEN: God, I love this country, I had forgotten, my *own* country! It made me weep on the bus. I pressed my cheek against the window and I felt the cool mountain air on the glass, and it made me cry even more.

Everyone takes in the orchard.

The orchard is all white. Rows and rows, like a tightrope, a string of bright white light.

---

12 Father in Punjabi.
13 In Punjabi, a term of respect for an elder, or grandfather.

KESUR: (*Quietly, slowly.*) Rows and rows of light. That strung from Gwalior Prison to the Golden Temple. Once a year we remember the release of Guru Hargobind Ji, the sixth Sikh Guru. (*For LOVELEEN.*) Imprisoned for his religion for twelve years, he had forgotten his way home. So the village lit candles from the prison to the Golden Temple. And that is why we celebrate the Festival of Lights. Happy Diwali, Lovely.

LOVELEEN: Papa it's not... (*To GUS about KESUR's memory.*) When did he...?

Oh god, my childhood. So pure. I woke up every morning to the same sound. Mummy whistling and starting the sprinklers. (*To GURJIT.*) We were happy back then, weren't we? In this light the orchard looks exactly the same, as if nothing has changed. (*Laughs.*) Oh, my orchard! After the dark autumn and stormy winter, you survived. Your branches come back stronger and full of life. But there is a stone that I carry and I cannot let the winter go.

GURJIT: ...and how strange, we cleared the rock and nursed the trees with our sweat... Now it's magnificent and the bank owns it all.

LOVELEEN: Mummy. I see our sainted mother, all in white, walking in the orchard. Do you see her Gus?

GURJIT: Where?

BARBRA: May the Lord bless you, mussi-ji.

LOVELEEN: (*Laughing.*) There's no one. It just looked for a moment, the way that branch curved in the shadow. Silly me...

> *PETER enters unnoticed, shabby and looking like an Indian intellectual with thick, black-rimmed glasses and a long, white kurta.*

Our beautiful orchard. White against blue.

PETER: (*In Punjabi.*) ਸਤਿ ਸ੍ਰੀ ਅਕਾਲ। (**Sat Shri Akal**[14]) auntie-ji. It's been a while. Barbra asked me to wait until morning, so when I heard the birds singing… I just came by to say hello and give you my blessings.

Pause.

BARBRA: (*To LOVELEEN.*) It's Peter. Prabhas Thiara.

PETER: Griesha's – may God be with him – Griesha's tutor. Am I so changed?

LOVELEEN: My Griesha…

LOVELEEN collapses, or perhaps runs to the locked door of her son's bedroom and tries to open it.

Griesha! My Griesha…!

LOVELEEN is overcome with grief and weeps in anguish, as if no time has passed since Griesha's death. Her reaction takes everyone aback. CHARLIE hears the commotion and enters unnoticed.

The family re-experiences a collective grief. Beat.

GURJIT: Yes, Lovely… that's enough. It's enough.

BARBRA: Peter, I begged you to wait until morning. Now look.

PETER: It is morning. (*To LOVELEEN.*) Forgive me. Forgive me, I just wanted to…

A long beat. LOVELEEN embraces PETER.

LOVELEEN: Griesha, my son, my only son… he was so young… not even seven…

---

14 Hello in Punjabi.

PETER sighs.

BARBRA: Mussi-ji, it was God's will.

LOVELEEN: My only son – drowned! And for what?! Peter, I ask you, for what…?! (*Quieter.*) And my Annie's asleep and I'm carrying on like this. Forgive me. (*Beat.*) Peter… When did you lose your good looks? You've aged more than me.

PETER: (*Referencing his long white kurta.*) On my way home a woman said I looked like "a smart ghost."

LOVELEEN: Back then you were a student, so full of life, and now you look dishevelled, you're wearing glasses… are you still a student?

PETER: I fear I will always be a student.

GURJIT: Our Bengali.

LOVELEEN: You're right Barminder. That's enough. Let's shut the lights.

CHARLIE shares a moment with KESUR, perhaps she goes to him, then she exits.

BARBRA: Actually, we have chores, mussi-ji. The tractor is acting up again, maybe you…

LOVELEEN: I think I'll lie down a little.

GURJIT: We can't expect her to jump in right away.

At some point PAUL has fallen asleep. He wakes up with a start.

PAUL: Ah! I was saying! A bird flew into the tailpipe yesterday! I hate to ask again, but I'm coming to you, hat in hand here –

BARBRA: We don't have it.

PAUL: That's all right – it'll turn up. Money always does. You remember last year, I thought I was finished, and then the city came and widened Valley Road. Had to buy a chunk of my front lawn. And! I've got my lucky lottery tickets right here. Something will come up… if not today, tomorrow.

KESUR: (*Inspecting Gurjit's underwear.*) Oye! Forgotten to wear your kacchera[15] again… will you ever learn?

GURJIT: Papa!

PAUL: All right then, time to get a move on. And tomorrow Lallie, really could we discuss a hundred dollars, a small loan.

GURJIT: My god! Just pawn all the jewellery in the house then!

LOVELEEN: Gus!

PAUL: No, I've uh, misstepped here.

LOVELEEN: Gus, apologize. The bank may be knocking down the door but this is still a community. My friend, whatever we can spare is yours.

LOVELEEN, PETER, PAUL, and KESUR exit. GURJIT, BARBRA, and YASH remain.

BARBRA: Yash, your mother has been sitting and waiting in the pickers' cabins. She won't go back until she sees you.

YASH: Waheguru[16] thank her for her sacrifice!

BARBRA: Have you no shame?

YASH: I'm just saying. The hassle is unnecessary.

GURJIT: Yash! You smell like a rest stop. Go home and take a shower.

---

15 Specific underwear worn by baptized Sikhs.
16 Sikh word for God. It means "Wonderful Teacher" in Punjabi.

YASH exits. With everyone gone, GURJIT and BARBRA finally relax. The room settles.

GURJIT, getting ready for bed, unwraps his turban and undoes his joora.[17] His long hair hangs freely. Beat.

BARBRA: I'm so tired, I could cry.

GURJIT: You know if a doctor suggests multiple cures for a disease, sooner or later common sense tells you it's incurable. I've come up with a thousand solutions to save this property but none seem to pan out. We could try again with Jaspreet Auntie in Vancouver. Their family is so very rich. Two Mercedes, BMW, their son goes to private school. But because I wear a turban and we work the land, they think they are above us.

BARBRA: Please Lord, remember us.

ANNIE enters unnoticed.

GURJIT: Oh hush now, don't cry... Now, if we sent our "cultured" new Lovely for a visit, she could impress them with her party romping. "Lallie." Our earthworm has turned into a lavish butterfly. But we can't afford the bus ticket to Vancouver.

BARBRA: We can't even afford the long distance charges!

They laugh through the tears.

(*Noticing Annie.*) Annie, why aren't you asleep?

GURJIT: (*Hiding tears.*) ... and what's this fluff in my right eye. You get old, your tear ducts overreact...

ANNIE: I can't sleep. I just can't. The bank. And the payments. What if we can't...?

---

17 A simple knot, how the hair is worn underneath the turban.

GURJIT: Don't fret, Annie. Lovely's so good with the orchard. One strong harvest and we'd have a chance.

ANNIE: Then why were you saying those awful things about her? Your own sister.

GURJIT: I'm not sure why I did it…

ANNIE: I believe you uncle. We all love you, respect you. But maybe some –

GURJIT: And then there was my speech in front of the bookcase, and even as I was saying it, I knew.

BARBRA: Perhaps not all thoughts need to be "announced."

GURJIT: Yes, I will, I do. Starting this second. But I do feel hopeful, girls. Listen to this Annie, last Wednesday I was at the gas station. I ran into that judge and he said we have right until the last minute to pay our debts.

ANNIE: Really?

BARBRA: That gives us…

ANNIE: Four months!

GURJIT: We will spend the money and have Lovely call your auntie in Vancouver. And if we must, we can speak to Michael about a loan. So you see! We have: a good harvest, Jaspreet Auntie, and a loan from Michael. A three-pronged attack, yes, we can't fail! I am so sure, I'll even swear on it. I swear on anything you like, this house, this orchard! I swear on my hope of happiness. Yes, here is my hand. Let's shake.

> *ANNIE and BARBRA put their hands in to shake. Then they all shake their bodies; their typical way of sealing a deal.*

I will not let us go to auction. Or else call me, call me, call me a liar and a thief! A Captain Hook!

ANNIE: Uncle!

GURJIT: A Captain Hook, I say!

KESUR enters.

KESUR: Gurjit Singh Basran, are you drunk? (*In Punjabi.*) ਸਵੇਰੇ ਸਵੇਰੇ ਐਂਵੇਂ ਭੌਂਕੀ ਜਾਂਦਾ। (**Hollering at all hours of the morning.**)

GURJIT: Drunk with purpose!

KESUR: Do you fear nothing? Get. Some. Sleep.

GURJIT: I will, I will. When will you see, I can help myself baba-ji. Peter Pan to the rescue. Goodnight, my girls. (*Beat.*) (*About to launch into a big speech.*) You know I am a man of the 50s –

ANNIE: Uncle!

BARBRA: Sleep, mama-ji.

KESUR: Gurjit.

GURJIT: Yes, all right. You're right. The crowd has won it. Second star to the right and on till morning.

GURJIT and KESUR exit.

ANNIE: I feel so much better. India was awful, but on the plane home… we *laughed*, Barbra. I haven't laughed that much in years. There's already colour in her cheeks again. She's eating more… Mom can fix this.

BARBRA:	You're right. For the first time in months, I can breathe again. (*Yawning*.) I'm so glad you're home, there's been no one to talk to. During church service there's always a sermon – like the thought of the week – and we sing songs, and the girls make jokes behind their hymnals... It's not so bad.

Pause.

But I go because of the sunlight, Annie. The way the sun streams through the stained glass and onto my face. It's red and warm – just like the sun in India. The church is the only place where it shines like that, and for a second I'm back home.

Annie, do you ever feel a hole inside of you? Like you should be somewhere else? And until you're there, a part of you will always be lonely? And no matter how happy you are... a little part of you will always be sad? Annie?

ANNIE has fallen asleep. PETER enters.

Shhh! She's asleep.

ANNIE:	No I'm not tired. Do you hear the bells mom? We left them in the trees for you. Uncle, does she hear them?
BARBRA:	Shh, shhh. My angel. (*In Punjabi*.) ਸੌਂ ਜਾ। **(Sleep.)**

BARBRA leaves ANNIE on the sofa sleeping.

Peter, I begged you.

PETER:	I'm sorry. I'm not a perfect man, Barminder. I only ask –
BARBRA:	No.

BARBRA exits, leaving PETER in the dark. PETER looks at ANNIE.

PETER:	Good night. My morning star. My springtime.

Orchard Interlude. Harvest.

> GRIESHA v.o.
> (*Whispers.*) Harvest.

The Basran Orchard, Summer 1969.

Summer in the orchard during harvest time. A rich soundscape fills the air. We hear the busy bustle of work. It is almost rhythmic. Boots on wooden ladders. Tractors. Buzzing of cicadas. Sprinklers. Fruit being separated from the tree.

It should feel hot like the midday heat of summer. The voice-over is distorted, far away in time.

> GRIESHA v.o.
> Sixteen, seventeen, eighteen…

> KESUR v.o.
> How many bins this year, Griesha?

~~~~

> GRIESHA v.o.
> Twenty-eight, twenty-nine, thirty…

~~~~

> CHARLIE v.o.
> The peaches look real good this year.

> LOVELEEN v.o.
> Thank you Charlie. It's our best harvest yet.

Act Two. Scene One.

> *The Basran Orchard, June, 1974. Two months later. The sun is about to set.*
>
> *The middle of the orchard. CHARLIE scrapes mud off her boots. YEBI stands at a distance, playing his guitar, with little success. YASH and DONNA sit apart. All are pensive.*

CHARLIE: (*Nonchalantly.*) Everyone thought I was dead. Guess I was always running away from that place.[18] When I was twelve years old I thought, this time I'm gonna make it out for good or come back in a luggage car. I brought two sandwiches and a map. Got as far as the main road and that's when I realized those nuns never taught me nothing. I couldn't read the map. So I followed the back trails like my káwa[19] taught me. But I took a wrong turn and ended up two provinces over. Life wasn't easy after that, I only knew how to be a rancher or a servant.

Then the Indian Rodeo came to town. Like I was calling for it, and it found me. I met this guy who taught me the horses and some of those tricks – started makin' good money too. Spent a lot of summers being an Indian cowgirl, travelling. Ended up all the way here, and then the rodeo went belly up. That's when old man Glenmore said, "Hey, I know you. You're Linda's kid." It turns out my rez was five miles away the whole time. I went home but mom had passed, and my káwa too.

I heard a lot of kids died running away, that I'm one of the lucky ones. But without the rodeo, who am I? I don't even have a birth certificate, so I just act young. I'm a lost generation, so they say.

---

18 Referring to residential school.
19 Maternal grandfather in Sylix..

> *CHARLIE takes a cucumber from her pocket and starts eating it.*

YEBI: I would love to ride in the rodeo.

CHARLIE: Sorry Yebi. I never seen a Jap ride in the rodeo.

> *Everyone enjoys the late afternoon air.*

DONNA: Feels weird to not be picking fruit this time of year.

YEBI: But how pleasant to play the mandolin. It's the little things.

DONNA: (*Touching up her makeup.*) That's a guitar, not a mandolin.

YEBI: To a cowboy in love it's a mandolin.

> *YEBI gets closer to DONNA.*

Giddy up partner!
Proud shadow of the cowboy.
Honest as sunset.

YASH: What was that?

YEBI: A cowboy haiku.

CHARLIE: Sorry Yebi. There ain't no such thing.

YEBI: And why not Miss Charlie? A haiku is a straight shooter. Just like a cowboy.

CHARLIE: Yebi, why do you love cowboys so much?

YEBI: Why does a cowboy love the endless horizon? It makes his soul stand taller. Take away his cattle, his land, but deep down he'd still know who he is. He'd still be proud.

CHARLIE: (*Moved.*) I've been riding rodeos my whole life, and no one's ever explained it to me like that.

YEBI: I used to see wild horses all the time when I was a kid. My camp[20] was on your rez.

CHARLIE: Guess the government wanted all the troublemakers together.

YEBI: Ah, the internment years. Fond memories. A lot of laughter and things…

DONNA: Whatever happened to that camp?

YASH: I heard they bulldozed it.

CHARLIE: Every last building. Just some concrete stumps now and the sun bleaching 'em dry. But those wild horses came back.

They share a beat.

Suddenly DONNA pretends to be attacked by an aggressive bee. She screams elegantly and swats it away, ending up next to YASH.

DONNA: Oh shoot. I thought I saw a bee. Yash, tell me more about India.

YASH lights a joint.

YASH: If you've got the cash, it's heaven.

YEBI: Personally I think I'm a cultured sort of fella. I've travelled. But what more does a man need besides the great Canadian sky and this mosaic of opportunity.

YASH: Uh, sure, dude.

DONNA: It must have been so exotic, with all the food and history and stuff…

---

20 Referring to Japanese Internment Camps. In Canada, the last camp closed in 1949.

YEBI: But sometimes I can't seem to figure it out, or, how they say, whether to live or to shoot myself. So to speak. It's very frustrating. That's why I always carry a pistol with me. You see, here it is.

YEBI shows his pistol, maybe he drops it. Everyone recoils.

CHARLIE: Well, that's enough for me. I'm going. (*Laughing.*) Everyone thinks they're so damn clever, but what does anyone really know? Who am I? No one can tell me.

CHARLIE exits leisurely.

YEBI: I want to address something… Speaking straight to the point, that is – I must get something off my chest. Fate seems to have had its way with me. There is no care for Yebisaka. I mean, yeah, suppose I'm wrong… Then why did I wake up this morning and find a millipede drowning in my milk? Like this… (*He gestures with both hands. Pause.*) Donna? (*Sighs.*) May I speak with you?

DONNA: Sure Yebi. Come on, what is it?

YEBI: If it's not too much trouble, in private.

DONNA: Okay, fine. But Yebi, could you be a dear and grab my parasol from the house? I don't want catch a tan.

YEBI: But the sun… the sun is setting, it's practically… yes, all right. Now I see a use for my pistol.

YEBI exits, strumming his guitar.

YASH: What a grueler!

DONNA: Oh god, one day he really is going to shoot himself!

YASH: Yeah.

A solemn beat. Then YASH and DONNA make out.

DONNA: Sometimes I get into such a state! Working at the fruit stand, I've grown sensitive Yash. See how smooth and white my skin is. Like a proper lady. (*Beat.*) But if you're lying to me Yash, I don't know what I'll do. My nerves would go to pieces.

YASH: Aw, come on peaches.

DONNA: You're all I can think about.

YASH: Yeah… (*Takes a puff.*) That's me.

DONNA: And you know so much. I bet I could ask you anything.

YASH: (*Listens.*) Shit, it's the Basrans and company.

DONNA impulsively puts her arms around him.

No, no, no, knock it off, will you. Don't want people to think we're going steady.

DONNA: That stuff stinks anyway.

DONNA makes a ladylike cough.

It gives me a headache.

Donna starts to exit.

YASH: Hey, peaches.

YASH tosses DONNA a peach from the tree. DONNA exits. YASH picks up his shears and starts pruning, as if he's been working all along. MICHAEL, LOVELEEN, and GURJIT enter.

MICHAEL: Decide. Make a Decision. Door one or door two. Am I speaking Japanese? Lallie, please, give me the green light. Really, it's decide or the auction block. Just give the word: Will you rent your land for RVers?

> GURJIT *examines the peach tree that YASH is pruning.*

LOVELEEN: How cosmopolitan to have a Pierogi House right here in town. Think of it, we've been to Poland and back and it's not even dinner yet.

GURJIT: Why does this tree never grow peaches?

MICHAEL: It's a simple yes or no. Lallie, say yes and be done with it.

GURJIT: We are exploring many avenues, Mr. Lopakhin.

MICHAEL: Yes, of course! Your interview for that city job. And what happened?

GURJIT: Yes, well…

MICHAEL: Ah come on, you rascal, out with it.

LOVELEEN: Our Barminder is feeding everyone peas and lentils morning, noon and night. I needed a break! Soon she'll be going into the field to pick weeds for saag.[21] (*Looking into purse for pills.*) Why did we come to Canada? Who cares! Here we are, back in the village, eating mustard greens for dinner. (*LOVELEEN drops some coins.*) There you have it…

YASH: I've got it, Lovely.

> LOVELEEN *finds her pills and takes one.* YASH *gathers the money.*

LOVELEEN: Thank you, Yash. And the Pierogi Polka Band! Those costumes! That singer!?

GURJIT: You didn't need to tip the accordion player.

LOVELEEN: You're no better, saluting those cheese buns.

MICHAEL: Look, all I'm trying to say –

---

21 A North Indian curry made of stewed bitter greens.

GURJIT: Yes, you're right. I have to learn restraint. (*To YASH.*) Why are you always here? Flip-flopping in front of me.

YASH: Your stories fill me with glee.

GURJIT: (*To LOVELEEN.*) This man must leave! Either him or me.

LOVELEEN: Go ahead Yash.

YASH: If you'll excuse me.

YASH exits.

MICHAEL: You know the Pandosy brothers heard about the property. They're circling like vultures.

GURJIT: Ridiculous!

LOVELEEN: Are those boys married yet?

MICHAEL: If the orchard goes to auction, that's it, the Pandosys will snatch it up for a song.

GURJIT: Our sister Jaspreet will be sending money. I'm sure of it. You were so good on the phone, Lovely.

MICHAEL: You see… yes! Yes, now that's something! How much? Five… ten thousand?

LOVELEEN: The amount doesn't matter. Even one thousand and we'd be grateful.

MICHAEL: One. Only one… that won't even cover the legal fees! (*Beat.*) Really, I can't. I have told you in the plainest English. *You. Will. Lose. Everything!* And still nothing registers.

LOVELEEN: Then let's have it! Go ahead, teach us, guru-ji.

MICHAEL: Teach? Every day I'm here telling you the same thing from the bottom of my heart. One thing. You must repurpose this land for RV rentals. Before time runs out and the orchard is repossessed. *Act! Take action!* And I promise you'll be rolling in money. You'll be saved.

LOVELEEN: This is the Basran family orchard, Michael. Not a parking lot! I'm sorry but a trailer park on an orchard, it's so cheap!

GURJIT: (*To LOVELEEN.*) The apple doesn't fall far from the tree.

MICHAEL: What did I ever…! What do you want me to do? Spill blood? Weep? Faint? You kill me. You are *killing* me. (*To GURJIT.*) You… you old bingo lady.

GURJIT: What's he saying?

MICHAEL: A bingo lady!

MICHAEL starts to exit.

LOVELEEN: (*Desperate.*) No, no, no, please don't go. Please, dear friend, I insist. Somehow you make everything better…!

MICHAEL: I don't see how.

GURJIT: (*Holding the shears, deep in thought to himself.*) If the captain overtakes the island, pirates running wild. Better trim the riff-raff.

GURJIT wanders off to prune the trees. LOVELEEN and MICHAEL are alone. They share a silence.

MICHAEL: You're different. Not in a bad way, like an old way, not that being old is bad, well it doesn't matter because you're not old, ah, I don't know what I'm –

LOVELEEN: Oh...! We've gotten so much wrong.

MICHAEL: You? Impossible.

> *Beat.*

LOVELEEN: This man I met in India, he was such a rush of life. He showed me the new Bombay. With streets so wonderfully loud, they swallowed you up. For years I was drowning in sulphur and salt air and it felt extraordinary. (*Laughing. Beat.*) And then he fell ill. We sold my apartment to pay his medical bills and then, he left me. For this young, breathless, uncracked thing... One day I bought a bottle of liquor and a pack of razors.

MICHAEL: Lallie...

LOVELEEN: And then like that, Annie appeared like a vision. I longed for the orchard, my true home. But I couldn't...

MICHAEL: When you were here, the orchard was thriving and full of life.

LOVELEEN: Today, express post from India. He asks for my friendship and begs me to return. Yes, what wouldn't a girl do for a little romance?

> *LOVELEEN takes a pill from her purse. GURJIT enters with peaches.*

GURJIT: Ahoy mateys! Back with treasures!

> *GURJIT hands out peaches.*

(*Aside.*) Did you bring up the loan?

LOVELEEN: (*Aside.*) No.

GURJIT: (*Aside.*) Oh, it looked so sombre.

MICHAEL: Whoa, this is one messy peach! Gooey!

> *MICHAEL struggles with his sticky hands. Does he wipe them on the grass? The tree?*

Ah! I saw a foreign film last night... very interesting.

LOVELEEN: Films! Other people's lives. And why don't you look at your own life? My dear friend... you should get married. It would suit you.

GURJIT: To be on the family way!

LOVELEEN: To our Barminder. Our darling Barbra.

MICHAEL: Yes.

LOVELEEN: A sweet girl. Hard-working girl. I see the way she looks at you. Yes, an engagement. How exciting!

> *KESUR enters, carrying GURJIT's coat.*

KESUR: Gurjit Singh Basran! (*In Punjabi.*) ਮੈਨੂੰ ਸੁਣਨਾ ਚਾਹੀਦਾ ਪਰ ਤੂੰ ਕਦੇ ਨਹੀਂ ਸੁਣਦਾ। **(You have to listen, but you never do. The sun goes and then you catch a cold.)**

> *KESUR puts the coat on GURJIT.*

GURJIT: Stop fussing! I can do it!!

KESUR: Even if I put the sweater in your hand, you still forget.

GURJIT: (*Overreacting.*) I said I can do it!! Just stop, let me be!

KESUR: What's the matter with him?

LOVELEEN: The city "cancelled" his interview.

KESUR: (*For his children, slowly.*) My first job was at the lumber mill. Long time ago. One time in the parking lot a big guy came up to me. He said, "Hey! Why are you here and wearing that turban?" Right close to me. I didn't know what to do, my English was small back then. Then a new guy came over there. And he say, "Why are you bothering him? So that's his religion. If you want to fight, come fight with me."

But I made sure I was never alone with that big guy again.

GURJIT: Well… that was a long time ago.

MICHAEL: (*Interjecting.*) You're right. We've forgotten about the buddy system.

LOVELEEN: (*Understanding.*) You haven't changed papa-ji.

KESUR: (*In Punjabi.*) ਏਹ ਕੀ ਕਹਿੰਦੀ ਆ? **(What's she saying?)**

GURJIT: She said, you're a young man of 60.

> ANNIE, BARBRA, *and* PETER *enter with pails of fresh-picked summer peas and fruit.*

Hullo, we see you!

ANNIE: We've been looking everywhere for you. No one's fixed the tractor. We can't move the fruit bins.

LOVELEEN: That's my fault, we got carried away at lunch. Oh, shoot, and the books, I forgot to look at them! (*To ANNIE.*) Forgive me, pretty please? I'll look at them tomorrow, cross my heart.

GURJIT: Oh, Lovely, the packing house said they would give us a very competitive price on our peaches.

MICHAEL: Oh that's the cake![22] They always say that.

---

22   That takes the cake.

LOVELEEN: Come, sit next to me, my darling. Why, how you've grown. If you only knew…

> *Everyone sits. BARBRA AND KESUR shell peas for dinner. GURJIT shells and eats the spoils. ANNIE cuts peaches with a pocketknife.*

MICHAEL: (*To PETER.*) The eternal student. Busy studying the ladies.

PETER: Why are you always here?

MICHAEL: You know, one day you'll be 50, senior's card in one hand, student card in the other!

PETER: I wish you'd give it a rest already.

MICHAEL: Ah look, what a sensitive soul! You should learn to woo a lady not be her playmate.

PETER: (*To LOVELEEN.*) Really, what is he doing here…?

MICHAEL: Okay okay, answer me one question, and I promise to back off. What do you think of me?

> *Everyone reacts to MICHAEL's challenge: "Here we go!" Groans. Laughter.*

PETER: I think you're a very rich man and soon you'll be a millionaire. (*Beat.*) In nature there are two animals. The predator and the prey. As humans we have evolved to see beyond these base instincts – (*To MICHAEL.*) but there are still some, the *ignorant neanderthals*, that insist on taking advantage –

ANNIE: Peter! Tell us about Communism.

LOVELEEN: No no, let's continue our debate from yesterday!

MICHAEL: And what was that?

GURJIT: Philosophy. "The Birth of the Free Man."

LOVELEEN: Yes exactly!

PETER: Yesterday. (*Pause.*) Yes, we talked about much, but arrived at nothing. In the Free Man, as you've called it, we agree there is the Individual and his Potential. But what is Freedom? How does the common man manifest an idea? What if there is a third component to the Free Man? And that is the *cultivation* of his unique Potential.

BARBRA: What difference does it make? All the same you die.

> *Everyone groans at BARBRA's doom and gloom.*

PETER: But what is the legacy you leave behind? And what is death? We know of five senses. All expire at death. But what about the gifts from the mind and the soul?! The opportunity to explore these gifts must be given in life, so the legacy of your mind can be left in death.

LOVELEEN: Peter, how clever you've gotten.

PETER: So I ask you again: what is Freedom? And I say, it is the ability to cultivate this *whole* person that is the *manifestation* of Freedom. And *that* is the birth of the Free Man.

MICHAEL: A beautiful thought.

PETER: And so, as legacies are left behind, the human race goes forward. *We* go forward. *Chasing* Freedom. But we must be given opportunity. And so there is a final gatekeeper to the Free Man, and that is Society. Society must *surrender* the right to opportunity. Because without the ability to access our Potential, we will never be free. And therefore, the Free Man cannot exist in an unjust society. (*Beat.*) In Canada, we live with a myth of equality!

> *Everyone audibly reacts to PETER's disruptive and possibly offensive idea.*

But we are stifled! Gratefully kneeling for any opportunity. Barely given room to exist as we are – Barminder has abandoned her religion!

BARBRA/ANNIE: Peter!

PETER: What if we went back to India? (*Beat.*) There we are not stifled. Our country is changing, no longer a pathetic third world nation, begging in the shadows. India could re-emerge a superpower! I believe it!

> *Everyone laughs at PETER's outlandish idea, except ANNIE.*

LOVELEEN: Peter, you are so silly.

GURJIT: Where does he get these grand ideas?

PETER: It's been three years since Trudeau opened up immigration. People are flooding into this country. Multiculturalism pervades every message. The left-leaning, common man pats himself on the back, thinking he has sacrificed and achieved this goal. But where is this free utopia they speak of? The liberal thinkers preach a mosaic, where every tile may shine as brightly as the next. But our stories are not in the classroom. Our medicine is not in the hospitals. Our philosophies – which have evolved tens of thousands of years – compared to this infant nation of only a hundred. But we are not refined enough, not advanced enough. And I ask you: where is the rigour of thought in that? (*To ANNIE.*) But I tell you, a better life is flowing into India.

> *Everyone has slowly stopped their activities, they now listen intently to PETER.*

PETER: In Delhi, I heard a man speak, Manmohan Singh. Society has given him opportunity, and his Potential is unleashed. He has these ideas! International trade will come to India. Yes, like him, if we invest our gifts into our *own* mother country, we will know true Freedom. If we *work*, a nation can shake off its darkness. Because I tell you, once our potential is liberated, no one can make us kneel.

Everyone is silent.

LOVELEEN: Well...

BARBRA: Peter, I... Really I can't believe you sometimes.

MICHAEL: Actually I know exactly what you mean. (*He discards his peach pit.*) It's about instilling work ethic. About investing the time. Just take me for example. I came from nothing. No one was knocking on my door. But I get up every morning at 5 a.m., I hustle and I've built my empire. And I believe any man can do the same. A fair shot to anyone, and that's what makes this country great.

PETER: Gus gets up every morning at 5 a.m. He can't get a job in a mailroom, and you have an empire. Your 5 a.m. started at the dawn of the colonies. Ours started in 1947 when the British finally let us buy an alarm clock.

MICHAEL: Come on! We've been blessed with soaring mountains and endless night skies. Surely, we were meant to live as giants!

PETER: Giants are for fairy tales.

GURJIT: People have welcomed us here, my boy. Perhaps you've forgotten. Remember the Nelsons? They gave you that bike, gave you rides into town to buy your books. You were like another son to them.

PETER: (*Beat.*) I feel I've gotten carried away. Nothing comes from this idle talk.

In the distance, YEBI is heard playing his guitar.

LOVELEEN: (*Pensively.*) There goes Yebisaka.

YEBI strums a bad chord. It does not sound good.

ANNIE: There goes Yebisaka.

Beat.

GURJIT: Ladies and gentlemen, the sun has set.

PETER: Yes.

> *Long pause. Everyone watches the sunset. They digest PETER's speech, each in their own way.*

GURJIT: (*In a subdued voice.*)
I see ranges of those hillocks, those forests
Moving with outspread wings from isle to isle,
From the unknown to the unknown.
With the flutter of starry wings
Darkness glimmers in the weeping night.[23]

ANNIE: (*Whispers.*) Uncle!

BARBRA: (*Whispers.*) Mama-ji, you promised.

GUTJIT: (*Quietly.*) Yes, all right, you're right. I am silent.

> *Everyone resumes their silent contemplation. Only KESUR is heard muttering Tagore's "Wild Geese" in Bengali. Beat.*
>
> *Suddenly a distant sound is heard, like a bell jangling and then sadly dying away.*

LOVELEEN: What was that?

MICHAEL: I... (*Pause.*) A blown engine... pesticide sprayer maybe.

GURJIT: Perhaps a bird. A small crow.

PETER: An owl...

LOVELEEN: It sounded just like...

KESUR: (*To LOVELEEN.*) When you were putting the silver bells in the trees, the day you slipped and your ladder crashed.

---

23 From Tagore's "Balaka" ("Wild Geese")

ANNIE: That's the day dad died.

BARBRA: Griesha loved those bells.

LOVELEEN: Come dear ones, let's go. It's getting dark. Annie, you have tears in your eyes. Don't be a sourpuss.

> *A Caucasian BOY enters, wearing dirty clothes. Because of his race, the BOY has more status than the Basrans. No matter what he does, there is nothing they can do.*

PETER: Everyone…!

BOY: Spare some peaches for a hungry boy.

GURJIT: Those aren't yours to take, young man.

BOY: What, gonna tell your boss on me?

MICHAEL: This is private property.

BOY: Sorry sir, I don't mean to be trespassing, just wondering if you're looking for some help?

MICHAEL: Ah no, this orchard doesn't belong –

GURJIT: No, we're not.

BOY: Keep your turban on, I'm not gonna steal your job.

ANNIE: Mom…

MICHAEL: Mind your manners, boy.

BOY: Nice peaches. But if you ask me, I'd watch out for mould. See this spot there…

> *LOVELEEN hugs the BOY. The BOY recoils.*

LOVELEEN: God bless you, child.

GURJIT: Lovely, stop it.

LOVELEEN: Wait! What if he gets hungry? Here, take this.

> LOVELEEN *takes bills from an inside pocket of her coat.*

ANNIE: Mom, that's twenty dollars!

BARBRA: Hey! We said you can't take those!

BOY: They were mine first…

> *The BOY presses a peach into BARBRA's shirt, staining it badly.*

(*Quietly, simply.*) …Rag-head.

PETER: Hey!

> *The BOY runs off. There is a stunned silence.*
>
> *Long beat.*

KESUR: (*Slowly, simply.*) You know, I love this little bracelet. Do you know the first kara was made of simple iron, so every Sikh person could afford it. Cheap little thing. But when I see others wearing it, I remember: I am part of a big religion, a big group. And you all wear the kara too. Let me see.

> *LOVELEEN, GUS, ANNIE, BARBRA and PETER all show their karas.*

So maybe here, the group is only us. But a small fry is still a potato.

> *Pause. The family almost comes together and then it fractures.*

BARBRA: Mussi-ji, I can't believe you. Twenty dollars?!

LOVELEEN: Oh god, I can't be trusted. You have to forgive me. Annie, you understand, don't you? I've been in India so long, I've forgotten how to do all this.

ANNIE: Yeah well, that's no surprise.

LOVELEEN: When I left, I didn't plan on staying away. I only took a little suitcase, a few clothes –

ANNIE: Are you kidding? You took everything.

LOVELEEN: It's all right, my darling, I'm back now.

ANNIE: No. We have nothing and you go out for lunch?! Why don't you do something? No one has done the pruning since you've been back. Everyone is too swept up by you and your adventures. Or have you forgotten? In sixty days we lose everything!

BARBRA: Annie, / stop it.

KESUR: (*In Punjabi.*) ਗੁੱਸੇ ਰਹਿਣ ਦੇ ਉਹਨੂੰ ਬਰਮਿੰਦਰ। **(Let her be angry,/Barminder.)**

ANNIE: I know dad is dead and Griesha is dead but I'm still here. I was here. Rotting. And you forgot me! (*Beat.*) Forget it.

ANNIE runs off.

PETER: I'll get her.

PETER exits after her.

LOVELEEN: (*Giving MICHAEL her purse.*) Take it, just take my purse. I can't be trusted.

MICHAEL: Of course.

Everyone starts packing up and heading back to the house for dinner.

LOVELEEN: And Barminder, if you'd given us five more minutes alone with Michael, you'd be a married woman!

BARBRA: Mussi! Really?!

MICHAEL: Ordellia, get to a nunnery!

GURJIT: Now, will you look at this! If I don't play pirates for a while, my hands start to shake.

MICHAEL: Oh nympth! In thy orbs are all my senses remembered.

LOVELEEN: I'm starving. Barbra, what's for dinner tonight?

BARBRA: My heart is still racing. That boy really frightened me.

MICHAEL: One last word on the subject, on the 22nd of August this orchard will be sold. Please, can I leave you all with that?

> *Everyone exits.*
>
> *In another part of the orchard, ANNIE runs on. She doubles over and tries to stop herself from crying. After a moment, PETER finds her. Their attraction for one another is driven by a meeting of the minds, an intellectual connection.*

PETER: Annie...

ANNIE: Don't.

> *Pause.*

Thank God for that boy! Barbra got so scared and now... we're alone.

PETER: Barminder. She's so afraid we'll fall madly in love. She follows us around everywhere. Some people. They are obsessed with this affliction of love. The very thought of attaining it consumes them. Keeps them from their life's work. But we... we are above love. And we choose to work.

ANNIE: The way you speak. And today, what an afternoon/ you were so...

PETER: Yes, not a cloud in the sky.

ANNIE: Do you understand what you've done to me, Peter? I used to love this orchard. All the people around us. This town. But when I hear you speak... and somehow I can't love this orchard like I did before.

PETER: All of India is our orchard. Your grandfather came to Canada with endless potential inside of him. I heard he had his degree in agricultural sciences, and now he is grateful to teach the apple trees.

Look out into your beautiful orchard. Your potential cannot be contained in these trees before us. And listen... do you hear the leaves rustling? That's your true self trapped in the wind.

Beat. ANNIE listens to the wind.

ANNIE: Peter... in Bombay? I told everyone I found mom right away... But the truth is she vanished. I had to stay in this sleazy hostel for weeks, I didn't know who to call... so I went to temple. But this Gurdwara was cool marble floors that I had only dreamed of. (*Beat.*) Do you remember those ratty old rugs and plastic tarp we used to pray under? Standing in that great hall, I felt so alone. But as soon as my forehead hit the carpet – kirtan[24] music swelling around me – I was safe. And I couldn't help it, I started to cry. It's been such an awful – when dad died and mom disappeared, suddenly I wasn't a daughter anymore. And when I took the prashad[25] in my hands, I prayed for mom to be well again and put an awful six years to rest. (*Smiling through tears.*) The Gurdwara was so beautiful, Peter. I'd never seen a real one.

PETER: Kesur still putting up that makeshift temple on the hill?

---

24 For Sikhs, an intonation-style singing of hymns, accompanied by musical instruments like the tabla and harmonium.
25 A scared pudding, consumed at Gurdwara.

ANNIE: Every month. Barbra stopped coming.

Beat.

PETER: Canada is behind the times. They take twice the space and leave no room for us. Not even a proper place to pray…!?

PETER grabs a handful of leaves.

Take back these leaves, and invest them in a country that wants us.

ANNIE: This is our country.

PETER: (*In Punjabi.*) ਪੂਰੇ ਦੇਸ਼ ਦਾ ਸਹਾਰਾ ਚਾਹੀਦਾ। **(You need an entire country's support.)**

ANNIE: I… I…

PETER: Annie, you could be everything. (*Quietly.*) Fuck this place. It doesn't deserve us.

ANNIE grabs a handful of leaves.

ANNIE: I confiscate these leaves… and so take back myself!

PETER: Take the keys to the gate and throw them in the creek! Walk away and be free!

ANNIE: The way you speak…!

PETER: I know I am not yet thirty, and yes, still a student – my kismat[26] I suppose – but crossing the ocean, I have seen the best and worst of both worlds. And my soul still remains light and full of hope.

ANNIE: (*Pensively.*) The moon is rising… I see it, Peter. Happiness. It's coming.

YEBI is heard in the distance, playing the guitar. The same sad song as before. Somewhere, BARBRA is looking for ANNIE.

---

26 Fate in Hindi and Urdu.

BARBRA: (*Offstage.*) (*Calling.*) Annie, where are you?

PETER: Maybe we won't live to see it. But what does it matter? Others after us will.

BARBRA: (*Offstage.*) Annie? Annie, where are you?

PETER: Ugh Barminder, will you please –

ANNIE: Oh! Let's go to the creek.

PETER: Perfect. (*In Punjabi.*) ਚੱਲ ਚਲੀਏ। **(Come on, let's go.)**

> PETER and ANNIE exit. BARBRA comes running in.

BARBRA: Annie! Hello?! Jesus!

> Silence. BARBRA secretly takes out a Gutka[27] and carefully unwraps it. She intones part of the Rehraas Sahib.[28] She has been reciting this prayer her entire life.

(*Reciting Gurbani.*)
ੴ ਸਤਿਗੁਰ ਪ੍ਰਸਾਦਿ ॥
ਰਹਰਾਸਿ ਸਾਹਿਬ ॥
ਸਲੋਕੁ ਮਃ ੧ ॥
ਦੁਖੁ ਦਾਰੂ ਸੁਖੁ ਰੋਗੁ ਭਇਆ ਜਾ ਸੁਖੁ ਤਾਮਿ ਨ ਹੋਈ ॥
ਤੂੰ ਕਰਤਾ ਕਰਣਾ ਮੈ ਨਾਹੀ ਜਾ ਹਉ ਕਰੀ ਨ ਹੋਈ ॥੧॥
ਬਲਿਹਾਰੀ ਕੁਦਰਤਿ ਵਸਿਆ ॥
ਤੇਰਾ ਅੰਤੁ ਨ ਜਾਈ –

(Ik Onkav Satgur Puvsaad. Rehraas Sahib.
Salok Mehelaa Pehlaa.
Dhukh Dharoo Sukh Rogue Payaa
 Jaan Sukh Thaam Na Hoee.
Thoon Kurtaa Kurnaa Meh Naheen
Jaan Hoan Kureee Naa Hoee.
Balhaaree Kudrat Vasia.
Tera Ant Na Jaaee –)

---

27 Daily prayer book for Sikhs.
28 Sikh Evening Prayers.

YASH: Barbra?

BARBRA: Holy shit! You scared me!

YASH: What are you doing here? (*Beat.*) I thought you were Presbyterian?

BARBRA: Go away Yash.

YASH: Is that Kesur's Gutka? He's gonna be so pissed.

BARBRA: Isn't there a girl in a back seat that needs you?

YASH: Seriously, what are you doing?

Beat.

BARBRA: I got baptized today.

YASH: Yikes.

BARBRA: After the service, I invited Susan and the girls back to the house, so we could celebrate and they could meet everyone. But the girls didn't want to come. They said it would be more fun to go to Kentucky Fried Chicken, which they know I can't eat because I'm vegetarian, and I said well can't we go to Denny's or something, but they really like the fried chicken and went without me and… When is it going to be enough? I wear their clothes. I eat their food. I pray to their God. I'm doing everything right! They lied, Yash! *They* did!

YASH: Their country. Their rules.

BARBRA: I know.

YASH: You could try this shaggy haircut. Worked for me.

BARBRA laughs a little.

It means you try harder.

BARBRA: Can you take the Gutka back?

> *YASH takes the book and starts to leave.*

Wait.

> *Beat.*

Take my kara too. (*She tries to remove her kara, it doesn't come off easily.*) It's weird, I've never taken this off... When I moved here, I thought I'd die and be reincarnated and have another chance at happiness, you know? Their country, their rules, right.

YASH: (*Imploring.*) I'm not the guy to talk you out of this Barbra.

> *BARBRA takes off her kara.*

Fine. Your secret's safe with me.

> *YASH takes the kara and leaves. BARBRA is alone.*

BARBRA: Guru-Nanak Ji, I want to disappear completely, into a new skin, a new life. So I guess what I'm asking is... please just let me go. Next time I look in the mirror, I don't want to see you staring back. In Jesus' name I pray. Amen.

Act Three. Scene One.

> *Inside the Basran House. August 1974. Two months later.*
>
> *LOVELEEN sits alone at a desk, wearing her old farm clothes and reading glasses. The house is quiet. She goes through paperwork for the auction.*

MICHAEL: An ominous time. But at last! The cherries have arrived! Congratulations Lallie.

LOVELEEN: Yes, twenty thousand dollars from the orchard, twenty thousand from Jaspreet.

MICHAEL: With four hours to spare.

LOVELEEN: (*Beat.*) …Will it be enough?

> *MICHAEL can't answer.*

You know, I did look at the books eventually. If I'd done a private sale –

MICHAEL: There'd be a little profit, but not much after you pay the bank and the interest and all the legal fees.

LOVELEEN: Enough to start over. I should have sold the damn thing months ago. Michael, I see you salivating like a donkey. If you want some just ask.

MICHAEL: Cherries are my favourite.

LOVELEEN: Help yourself. Best harvest in the valley.

> *MICHAEL gorges himself on cherries, eating around the pit like an apple.*

MICHAEL: Forty thousand dollars is… very respectable.

LOVELEEN: The Pandosy brothers are vultures. Michael, why are you eating that cherry like that? You look ridiculous.

MICHAEL: The pit is unsettling. What if I swallow it? I see how those other guys do it. Put the whole thing in their mouth and just spit out the seed like a macho man.

LOVELEEN: We must all join the real world eventually.

MICHAEL: I suppose.

> *MICHAEL throws a cherry in the air and catches it in his mouth. Unfortunately, the cherry gets stuck in his throat. He gulps. LOVELEEN looks at a letter.*

LOVELEEN: A letter from Jaspreet. If we lose, she wants the money back. Sisters! We'd be broke. And homeless.

MICHAEL: You will win.

> *MICHAEL makes a hairball sound.*

LOVELEEN: What's the matter?

MICHAEL: It's stuck. (*Makes hairball noise.*) Th' stupid cherry's stuck.

LOVELEEN: Stop fooling around.

MICHAEL: (*Makes hairball noise.*) It won't go down and it won't come out.

LOVELEEN: Slap your chest.

MICHAEL: Am I turning blue?

LOVELEEN: Throw yourself on something!

> *MICHAEL does.*

Michael! Michael! Oh god, are you choking? Talk to me!

MICHAEL: Losing. Oxygen.

LOVELEEN: Oh god! Hang on!

> *LOVELEEN slaps his back. MICHAEL spits out the cherry. It sadly rolls across the floor as he gasps for air.*

Holy shit.

MICHAEL: Holy shit! I almost died! Right here, like that – (*He makes a death pose.*)

LOVELEEN: Oh god, that face you made!

> *They both laugh hysterically.*

MICHAEL: How much do I owe you doctor?

LOVELEEN: Deduct it from our tab.

MICHAEL: That you can't pay!

LOVELEEN: All loans forgiven at death.

MICHAEL: It's the sale of a lifetime! Blowout prices! Everything must go!

LOVELEEN: Sign me up!

> *LOVELEEN writes MICHAEL's name on the deed.*

MICHAEL: (*Laughing.*) Don't write on that – that's a legal document. I think I peed a little.

LOVELEEN: Let's make it official!

MICHAEL: It feels very official. Moist.

LOVELEEN: (*Playfully writing.*) Michael Lopakhin can buy the orchard.

MICHAEL: Lovely handwriting.

LOVELEEN: (*Seriously.*) So take it.

> *Beat.*

BARBRA: (*Offstage.*) We're back!

LOVELEEN: When you were a little boy, I did a favour for you once, do you remember?

MICHAEL: (*Heartfelt.*) Yes.

LOVELEEN: I can't leave them with nothing.

> MICHAEL *suddenly understands.*

MICHAEL: This… this would ruin everything.

> Beat.

LOVELEEN: (*Lightly.*) I'm being silly! This afternoon heat is getting to me!

> LOVELEEN *leaves the deed on the desk.* BARBRA *and* DONNA *enter, followed by* ANNIE, *with bags of food and party supplies.* DONNA *wears a natural-looking blonde wig.*

BARBRA: Why we're having a party tonight is beyond me.

DONNA: I melted all the ice!

BARBRA: Donna!

DONNA: I'm sorry! I'm sorry!

ANNIE: What did that salesman want now?

LOVELEEN: Today my heart is so heavy. Where's Yash?

ANNIE: Who knows.

DONNA: Who cares!

BARBRA: He's getting the drinks.

> KESUR *is suiting up* GURJIT. *Fixing his turban so it's perfect.* GURJIT *is anxious to speak in front of the judge, who is Caucasian.*

KESUR: Whatever happens at the auction is God's will. And we must trust in the Almighty Lord. That is the most important thing.

YEBI approaches ANNIE.

YEBI: Annie! Look, I learned how to make an F.

YEBI strums, it's awful. He exits.

ANNIE: (*Calling after him.*) Yebisaka, I don't think that sounds right!

LOVELEEN: (*To MICHAEL.*) August 22, calling in all debts!

MICHAEL: Gus, I'll meet you outside.

MICHAEL exits with a stack of papers.

GURJIT: They said I'll have to speak to the judge before it can all proceed. (*Worried.*) Can you hear my accent?

LOVELEEN: (*Sincerely.*) You don't have an accent, brother.

Car honks again.

GURJIT: That's my cue!

Act Three. Scene Two.

> *Inside the Basran House. Later that evening. A country folk band plays offstage.*
>
> *Only KESUR, PAUL, and CHARLIE are inside, shooting the breeze. KESUR, wearing Indian dress, passes out soda pop to PAUL and CHARLIE. Outside, the party is in full swing.*

PAUL: (*Taking a glass from KESUR.*) Thank you my friend, thank you! Ah! What a night. You know I've had two heart attacks, can't dance like I used to. But like my father said – God rest his soul – "prance or not, you have to swish your tail!" He loved a good joke. Did you know my dad said us Andersons come from an ancient breed of stallions? How's that for good ole Canadian stock!

> *ANNIE and PETER enter, deep in one of their debates.*

ANNIE: You can't deny that he's opening up immigration in an unprecedented way. The face of this country is changing, Peter. I have hope.

PETER: Oh here we go.

ANNIE: The man gave birth to multiculturalism!

PETER: Yes, our brown brothers and sisters are flooding into this country, but he is blind to nativism, the fear of the other. And fear is a powerful thing.

ANNIE: So we give up on Canada? What if we cultivated our own potential? *Demanded* our right to opportunity.

PETER: Well... then...

ANNIE: Oh my god! I got you! (*Beat.*) I wish uncle was back already. How are you so calm?

PETER: "Reason before passion."

PAUL butts into their conversation.

PAUL: Are you Trudeau? That's Trudeau, isn't it? You know, that man said if the country needs more money, we should just march across to the bank and print some more. Imagine that.

ANNIE: You follow politics?

PAUL: You bet! And things have been so tight, I might have to test Trudeau's theory. Tomorrow I owe the mechanic $310. (*Feels in his pockets with alarm.*) Oh god. I've lost my lotto tickets. Oh, no, no, no – ah, there they are! Slipped in the lining. Yes, here they are.

BARBRA passes through.

BARBRA: The musicians sound good. I don't know how we're going to pay for them.

BARBRA exits.

PAUL: You know I like that Trudeau guy, he's a bit of a passion fruit, but look, all that immigration stuff, we gotta do it responsibly. This has always been a tight-knit community. I mean you guys fit right in.

PETER and ANNIE share a discreet look.

I just don't want a them-and-us situation. (*Falls asleep, snores, wakes himself up.*) Boil it all down, it's about preserving a way of life. I'm telling you, this country is headed for a mess. How are we going to fix it?

CHARLIE: Ask someone with the owner's manual.

LOVELEEN and YASH enter.

LOVELEEN: Where is Gurjit? He should have been back hours ago. The band came late, the guests arrived early, something's not right... Well, never mind now.

CHARLIE: Perhaps the auction never happened.

LOVELEEN: This music is so loud. I can't think straight.

>*CHARLIE yells to the band outside, "Take a break, boys!" and exits.*

YASH: Time for your pills, aunti-ji.

LOVELEEN: Not tonight.

YASH: Lovely, can I ask you something? If you go to India again, take me with you. (*In a subdued voice.*) I know I don't have to tell you... this farm life, I'm in the pind[29] all over again. I want to make something of myself... Please, you have to take me with you.

>*CHARLIE enters with her lasso. BARBRA follows behind her. YEBI wanders in sometime during CHARLIE's speech.*

CHARLIE: Ladies and gentleman, can I have your attention, please! I'm Charlie Isaac, your MC for the evening and resident Rodeo Queen! (*Everyone cheers.*) Are you ready for a show?! (*More cheering.*) Now I wouldn't be much good without my lucky lariat. First I gotta build my loop.[30] Let's get this old girl going! On the count of three, can I get a Yee-Haw – one, two, three!

ALL: Yee-haw!!

>*CHARLIE swings her lasso high into the air. Everyone cheers!*

---

29 Village in Punjabi.
30 To prepare a lasso for a throw.

CHARLIE: There she goes! But! What is the hardest animal to catch? Not a buck or a mad steer. No... It's a simple, wild, Basran tenderfoot.

> *ANNIE gets up, ready to play her part. She hides from CHARLIE behind a chair.*

Let's see a little catch-as-catch-can[31] and... What lovely weather we're having, isnt' it?

ANNIE: Yes isn't it marvellous!

CHARLIE: I'd know that tenderfoot anywhere! Here we go folks, one, two, three!

ALL: Yee-Haw!!

> *ANNIE prances like a deer and CHARLIE ropes her. Everyone cheers!*

CHARLIE: Ah ha! Caught the little calf, clear as day!

PAUL: Well I'll be damned! Miss Charlie?

CHARLIE: Yes?

PAUL: I'm in love with you.

PETER: A regular old horse!

CHARLIE: And for the grand finale, we need a volunteer.

PAUL: Me, oh me!

CHARLIE: As you know, my speciality is calf-ropin'. Let's see if we can beat my record! Dear scholar, will you keep time? (*PETER nods.*) Paul, you ready?

PAUL: Yee-Haw!

> *CHARLIE hog-ties PAUL like a calf, as party guests count: one, two, three...*

---

31 The roper can catch the cattle any way they choose.

CHARLIE: (*Throwing both hands in the air.*) Time!

PETER: Ten seconds! (*Or whatever the actor can manage.*)

CHARLIE: All right, now if you'll show your appreciation.

    CHARLIE takes off her hat to collect money.

PAUL: Oooh, that hurt a little.

LOVELEEN: (*Circling CHARLIE's head with money and dropping it in the hat.[32]*) Thank you Charlie.

YEBI: (*With CHARLIE's lasso in hand.*) In the spirit of cowman-ship, I've been cooking up a new trick. What do we have here, the mother of all loops, the Mother Hubbard.[33] But!! What if it was on fire!?

    YEBI whips out a lighter.

ALL: NO!!!

BARBRA: The pies are served!

    Everyone begins to exit.

PAUL: I seem to be a little stuck, if someone could untie me.

    LOVELEEN, YASH, BARBRA, and PETER remain. The room settles.

LOVELEEN: What time is it? Still no Gurjit. No Michael. I don't understand, where are they? Well it doesn't matter. By now the house is either sold or not sold, or the auction never took place – why do they keep us in misery! Yash, maybe I will have a small something.

---

32 A South Asian custom intended to bless someone.
33 A very large loop or lasso.

YASH: Of course.

YASH gives LOVELEEN one of her pills.

LOVELEEN: Give me a few of them.

YASH does so, and then exits.

BARBRA: Uncle had the highest bid. I'm sure he did.

PETER: (*Sarcastic.*) Well if you're sure.

BARBRA: Once they realize the property's in the land freeze, no one will want this stupid orchard. Lord hear us.

LOVELEEN: (*Covering her face with her hands.*) Oh, today I learn my fate.

PETER: "Mrs. Lopakhin…"

BARBRA: Yes, you ancient student. What, kicked out of another university?

LOVELEEN: He's just playing Barminder. This "you and Michael" drama has got to end. He's a nice enough young man. Well if you're up for it…

BARBRA: Of course I am – I do think about it. Very seriously, mussi-ji.

LOVELEEN: Then marry him and get it over with! I don't understand you girls.

BARBRA: Well I can't propose to myself! It's been months of him coming over and awkward silences and I think he's about to and then… And now everyone is talking to *me*. But what about him? He either says nothing or starts rambling. If I had a little money, I'd have left by now.

PETER: Back to India?

BARBRA: Missionary work.

PETER: A beautiful life!

BARBRA: Shouldn't you be studying somewhere? Always so clever. (*Softly and tearfully.*) How ugly you've gotten Peter. The light has been sucked right out of you. (*To LOVELEEN, the tears gone.*) The only thing I want is to be of service. True service.

YASH enters.

YASH: Yebi broke the bicycle!

YASH exits.

BARBRA: Yebisaka is still here! Why is he riding around in the dark?!

BARBRA exits.

LOVELEEN: Please. Leave her alone, Peter. She's suffering. And upset enough, so be nice to her.

PETER: Suffering? She's too busy sticking her nose in everyone's business to be suffering. All summer, I couldn't get a moment's peace. Afraid that Annie and I would have a "romance." The frivolity. When we have made an oath. We are *above* love.

LOVELEEN: Above love? And what, I am below it? Where's Michael? They should be back by now. Is the property sold or not? I think of it and... I'm drowning. Peter, rescue me, do something, *say* something... (*Pause.*) For God's sake, speak!

PETER: The house is either sold or not. And no matter the outcome, it was foretold long ago. So keep calm, auntie-ji. For once in your life, look truth straight in the eye and be at peace.

LOVELEEN: What truth? What peace? You see truth and I see *untruth*. So I am blind, I wish to see nothing. You see a problem and you *decide*. But tell me, my dear boy, isn't that because you're young? These problems you find – you haven't survived them. And so you look boldly forward. Because you don't see, these actions will cost you *something*. So you are braver than us. More ethical, more intelligent. Then be generous. Be generous to me. Spare me. I was born in this house. My father planted these trees. My beautiful mother... And without this orchard, what am I? My son drowned here. You were the last person to see – have pity on me, my dear boy...

LOVELEEN weeps.

PETER: You know you have my sympathy.

LOVELEEN: Oh, can you say that differently? Don't look at me like that Peter. Don't. I love you like my son. If you want Annie's hand, just ask and I'll give it to you. But, but you must finish your studies. Fate tosses you this way and that. You have no roots, no home. And for the wedding, this beard... can't you get it to grow?

PETER: Superficial beauty does not interest me.

Beat. LOVELEEN changes the mood effortlessly. She takes out a letter.

LOVELEEN: Another letter from Bombay. I got one yesterday and then today... the same thing. He's sick. Again. And he begs me to return. And I have to, I *must*... (*Beat.*) Why that face, Peter? So stern. Bacha,[34] what do you want me to do? He's sick. Alone and unhappy. Who will take care of him? Give him his medicine, make sure he doesn't act the fool. The truth is... I deserve him. I do. He's a stone around my neck and he will drag me to the bottom, but I don't care. Peter. Don't. Don't you dare judge me.

---

34 Affectionate term for child in Punjabi.

PETER: The man robbed you. (*Grabbing the letter.*) Continues to rob you –

LOVELEEN: Stop it. Stop speaking that filth. I won't…

PETER: He's a crook, you're the only person –

LOVELEEN: Enough!

PETER: No! – in the whole world that doesn't see it! He's a thief. A gold-digging, lying, / motherf – !

LOVELEEN: Prabhas! You're 28 years old, you, you're just a / child, a –

PETER: So be it!

LOVELEEN: Not so be it. A *man*, at your age, learn to be a man. You have to let yourself *live*! To understand love, to understand *why* people love and fall in love. Yes, yes I said it. Enough's enough, Peter. This dream of being a political revolutionary is for schoolboys.

PETER: (*Shocked.*) I'm sorry, what?

LOVELEEN: "I am above love." You are not Mahatmaji.[35] To have never kissed a woman –

PETER: (*Horrified.*) What / what are you saying?

LOVELEEN: / – at your age, no lover!

PETER: I won't listen to this. I – it's everything that's between us / – we're finished.

LOVELEEN: Peter, you will listen to me! You are my *son*!

PETER: …What?

LOVELEEN: *Like* a son. I meant like a son.

PETER: Stop this! This pressure to play pretend with you.

---

35 A reference to Gandhi, commonly referred to as Mahatmaji.

LOVELEEN: I forgot myself, Prabhas… (*Beat.*) Silly Peter, please, please come back.

> *PETER runs out of the room. Then offstage, there is a CRASH!*

What was that?

> *ANNIE runs in.*

ANNIE: (*Giggling.*) Peter fell off the porch!

> *ANNIE runs out.*
>
> *In another room, PAUL makes an announcement.*

PAUL: (*Offstage.*) Ladies and gentlemen! An announcement! The city is considering my land to build a communal mailbox. A toast my friends! To the good life that might await!

> *The guests toast.*
>
> *ANNIE enters with a bruised PETER.*

ANNIE: Peter had a little slip.

LOVELEEN: Peter. Such a handsome boy. Forgive me, my friend. Dance with me.

> *PETER dances with LOVELEEN. PETER quietly hums a melancholy Punjabi folk song to her, perhaps "Jind Mahi."[36] ANNIE watches from a distance and then exits.*
>
> *KESUR enters and takes the cane by the door. YASH enters.*

YASH: Why the cane, granddad?

---

36 "Jind Mahi" by Asa Singh Mastana.

KESUR: I don't feel well. (*Beat.*) It used to feel like a party even though it was just the family. It was enough people to dance and laugh. And now look, we have to invite the whole town just to play music. But who is laughing? The body gets weak somehow.

> *KESUR collapses onto the floor, spilling a tray of snacks.*

LOVELEEN: Dad!

> *BARBRA comes rushing in.*

KESUR: I'm okay. I'm all right. No need to fuss.

BARBRA: Oh my God. (*Running over.*) Oh my God, baba-ji!

KESUR: I just lost my feet for a moment. (*In Punjabi.*) ਦੇਖੋ, ਮੈਂ ਠੀਕ ਆਂ, ਮੇਰਾ ਫਿਕਰ ਨਾਂ ਕਰੋ। **(Don't make a fuss. Better already.)**

> *ANNIE runs into the room.*

ANNIE: In the backyard! A man said the orchard has been sold!

LOVELEEN: Sold. To who? Who bought it?

ANNIE: He didn't know.

LOVELEEN: Go and get him!

ANNIE: He left!

YASH: It was Billy Abbott. Forget him auntie. He never liked us.

KESUR: Gurjit still not back. It gets dark, the air gets chilly / – and he took his light jacket.

LOVELEEN: I feel like I'm going to die. Papa, if the property is sold, where will we go?

KESUR: Wherever God takes us.

LOVELEEN: You're trembling, papa. What's the matter? You should go to bed.

KESUR: And if I go to bed, who will look after the guests?

LOVELEEN: Yash, go run after Billy for me.

YASH: She said he left! Ha!

LOVELEEN: Yash, what is wrong with you?

YASH: (*Hiding tears.*) Something in my eye. One Mr. Yebisaka. Wherever he goes, bad luck follows. I need a drink.

YASH exits. PAUL enters in a festive mood.

PAUL: There you are! My lady, one dance, a two-step!

LOVELEEN: Paul, I couldn't help but hear your announcement. I was wondering... if we should need some money in the near future, if you would considering loaning us –

PAUL: Ah, wish I could but I got Brenda's tuition bills to pay.

LOVELEEN: (*Confused.*) Our families have always looked out for each other.

PAUL: Yeah, well... I'm pulling down the pickers' cabins in the fall. Come by, I'll pay you for that.

LOVELEEN: Thank you my friend. That's very kind of you.

PAUL whisks her away.

The room is empty. Only KESUR sits alone. In another room, CHARLIE does more rodeo tricks.

CHARLIE: (*Offstage.*) Another disappearing act for you fine folks. Keep your eyes on the lasso. One, two –

GUEST: (*Offstage.*) (*Hostile.*) Why don't you disappear?!

DONNA waltzes in alone. Shortly after, YASH wanders in.

DONNA: The music orders me to dance – what's a lady to do? Ah, the whole world is spinning and my heart is beating so fast. And Kesur, did you hear? Danny Bennett said I looked like a blossom. Took my breath away!

KESUR: What he say?

DONNA: That I was a blossom!

YASH: Oh god. What a line.

YASH wanders off, as YEBI enters.

DONNA: (*To YASH.*) Because people can see I am a delicate girl. And I love *poetry*!!

YEBI: You are drunk, Miss Donna.

DONNA: Like a blossom!

DONNA drapes herself on YEBI.

YEBI: If I may, you might look on me like a spineless bug, and maybe you're right, but – stop that – I speak from the heart, and… (*In Japanese.*) さなえちゃん、さなえちゃんは俺の心を嵐みたいに振り回すから正直に言わせてもらうけど、**(Senae, I say this because you have whipped my heart around like a storm –)**

DONNA: Don't speak like that here.

YEBI: (*In Japanese.*) さなえちゃん、気取ってるよ。髪型はいつも派手だし。洋服も。友達として言うけど、バカにされてるよ。 **(You put on airs. Your hair is always so flamboyant… your clothes – I tell you as a friend, Senae. People think of you as a fool!)**

YEBI pulls off DONNA's blonde wig.

DONNA: I look like a fool?! (*In Japanese.*) よく言うわよ！自分はどうなのよ？えびさかのエビ！エビのカウボーイ！ **(How can you say that! Yebisaka, the shrimp! The cowboy shrimp.)**

YEBI: (*In Japanese.*) 俺たちは自分の身分を忘れちゃいけないんだよ。**(We have to remember our standing.)**

DONNA throws a glass of water at YEBI.

DONNA: No, no, I'm dreaming now.

YEBI: (*Sighs.*) (*In Japanese.*) あーしかし、不幸というものはいつも俺を探し出す。古い親友みたいにね。やあ、不幸さん。**(Then again… Misfortune seems to find me like an old friend. Hello, "Mr. Misfortune.")**

BARBRA enters.

BARBRA: (*To YEBI.*) Are you still here? Nice manners you've got – sorry Donna – first you break a bicycle, then you sneak away and leave it in pieces, and now you're roaming around like it never happened. And who even invited you?!

YEBI: My apologies for the accident. But I work here too and have a right to be at the party like anybody else.

BARBRA: Work?! Donna, look around, would you ever guess in a million years that we have a *handyman?!* You break more things than you fix!

YEBI: No matter if I'm clumsy – I am sorry about that, really – but I work hard. And if I choose to eat, drink, ride a bike or walk around the house, I have earned the right… and who are you to judge me? Is your name on the checkbook?

BARBRA: How dare you say that to me! Test me again Yebi, I won't be so generous. After all I do around here! Get out. Get the hell out of here!

YEBI: If I may, no man wants to marry a sailor's mouth, Miss Barbra.

BARBRA: Get out! GET OUT!

YEBI goes to the door. BARBRA follows him.

Mr. Misfortune! I don't want anything to do with you. Don't step foot in this house again!

YEBI: She doesn't have the authority…

BARBRA: Oh really?! (*Taking the cane.*) Here then!

YEBI: Oh no no no no no.

BARBRA chases YEBI offstage with the cane. DONNA follows. BARBRA swings the cane, as MICHAEL enters.

MICHAEL: AH! And hello to you too.

BARBRA: Oh shit! Shoot… I'm sorry, oh God! Sorry.

MICHAEL: Next time you gotta buy me a drink first.

BARBRA: Oh dear, did I hurt you?

MICHAEL: No blood.

BARBRA: Thank goodness.

MICHAEL: But there is a little… *bump*.

PAUL enters, followed by LOVELEEN, ANNIE, and YASH.

PAUL: Michael! You smell like smokes and cheap whiskey, and so do we.

LOVELEEN: You're back. What took so long? Where's Gurjit?

MICHAEL: He's locking the truck, he'll be right in.

LOVELEEN: And… What happened? At the auction. What did they – speak for God's sake!

MICHAEL: It was all over by four. Then the truck broke down and we had to wait at the station bar until it was fixed... Ugh! I have to sit.

GURJIT enters.

GURJIT: Papa. Is there any subjee?[37] I haven't eaten at all today. Oh God...

LOVELEEN: Gus, my little brother, tell us, quick before I –

In another room, CHARLIE makes an announcement to the party guests.

CHARLIE: (*Offstage.*) The BBQ is ready!

The party guests cheer.

GURJIT: Never mind the food, papa.

PAUL: First tell us! How did the drama unfold today?

BARBRA: Has the orchard been sold?

GURJIT: Yes.

Beat.

LOVELEEN: And who bought it?

Pause.

MICHAEL: Me.

LOVELEEN is overcome.

Yes. I bought it! Ahhh! Am I dreaming?! A moment please, ladies and gentlemen, I want to remember this moment clearly. I don't have the words... (*Laughs.*) This afternoon, I didn't know what game you were playing at, Lallie, I must admit, but –

GURJIT grabs deed.

---

37 General term for a curry dish in Punjabi.

GURJIT: Is this your signature?

LOVELEEN: Yes.

MICHAEL: Well, when we got to the auction the Pandosy brothers were already there. Those damn sharks. Gus had the $40,000 ready to bid. But this deed was burning a hole in my pocket. The auction was about to start, the judge hit his gavel, one, two and I saw the window closing, the hope of a future – and before he could bang three, I said, "STOPP! The orchard has already been sold!" Well the Pandosy brothers didn't know what to think. So I showed them the deed. Signed, sealed. And not a damned thing they could do about it! The looks on their faces.

GURJIT: How could you Lovely? Sell our orchard to this monster.

LOVELEEN: I didn't.

GURJIT: How much did you sell it for?! Hmmm? How much did this snivelling businessman give you?

MICHAEL: I'll give you forty-five. It is in the land freeze after all, more than a fair price.

GURJIT: Congratulations! You sold this family for forty-five thousand dollars. Bravo!!

LOVELEEN: I thought, I thought –

ANNIE: You signed this?!

LOVELEEN: No. With this money – we have money now. We can just – start over and, it'll be all right.

GURJIT: You can't just waltz in here after *five* years. For *five* years, where the hell were you?! You had no right.

YASH: Here Lovely, take one of your pills.

GURJIT: No no no pills!

> *Hearing the commotion, CHARLIE rushes in.*

No. More. Pills!

> *Pause.*

I'm going to take a shower.

> *GURJIT exits.*

MICHAEL: Yes. It's mine. The orchard is mine!

> *YASH exits.*

Oh god, pinch me – if this is the liquor talking, God help us. (*Stomps his foot.*) Don't you think of laughing at me! Old man, if you could see me now! I'm flying!! See how pathetic little Michael, the illiterate, beat-down boy, who ran barefoot in the winter – see how he bought the most beautiful place on earth! Yes, I bought the place where my father and grandfather worked like peasants, planting seeds! Weren't allowed to shower in the house. I must be asleep, I must be dreaming.

> *BARBRA takes the keys off her chain and throws them at MICHAEL's feet.*

You throw these keys to shame me? (*Jingles the keys.*) Ah never mind that. Come on why has the music stopped?! Play me something, something happy!

> *CHARLIE and KESUR share a look. KESUR slowly exits, BARBRA goes with him.*

Just wait, all of you! You watch how Michael Lopakhin takes an axe to this cherry orchard and cuts these old logs down! We're gonna build an army of parking pads, and our children and grandchildren will grow up here and see a new life! A better life! For God's sake, MUSIC!

LOVELEEN: What have I done?

LOVELEEN weeps.

MICHAEL: Lallie, my dear friend. Don't cry.

LOVELEEN: Why did you do it?

MICHAEL: (*Crestfallen.*) No, no no, you signed the deed. I thought… Isn't this what you wanted? Ah, you stubborn woman, why didn't you listen to me? I thought… Why these tears, hm? Come on, can't we get past this… this unhappy life!

CHARLIE: That's enough, sir, she's weeping. So let her.

MICHAEL: No! I don't desire it. I am the new landlord here, here comes the master of the house, the master of the cherry orchard! (*Bumps into a table, glasses fall.*) Not a problem, I can pay for it.

Everyone exits. ANNIE cleans up the mess, then starts to leave.

LOVELEEN: Annie, my angel. Please, don't go. You can go back to school now, any school, a great school. This place, this orchard, it's only ghosts.

ANNIE: Gus-Uncle won't say it so I will. (*Beat.*) Get out. Pack your things and leave. I mean it. Go! You don't get to decide what's best for us. You're selfish, you sneak around and you lie –

LOVELEEN: I wasn't Annie. I promise, this time I wasn't, I wasn't being selfish.

ANNIE: I know Griesha is gone, but when are you coming back? Because you're not here. Please mom… I know you can do it. I remember this woman you used to be, she was so strong.

LOVELEEN: I see her Annie, but she is so far away.

ANNIE: Christ, snap out of it!

LOVELEEN: Stop pushing me! Please!

Long pause.

ANNIE: I can't. I can't do this anymore.

ANNIE walks away.

LOVELEEN: Annie. Please honey.... Don't leave me here. Annie.

Orchard Interlude. Dreaming.

>   GRIESHA v.o.
>   (*Whispers.*) Dreaming.

The Basran Orchard, Autumn 1969.

*Sunset. The air is peaceful.
That time of day that stretches on forever,
but only lasts a moment.*

*This interlude can be scored with music.
Gentle sounds of KESUR reciting the holy book
and GRIESHA's laughter.*

*There are no bodies onstage. A makeshift canopy hangs
from the trees. Underneath the canopy, a patchwork of
rugs cover the grass. Placed on the rugs is a single apple
box with the unwrapped Gutka on top, creating an altar.
Shoes and sandals surround the edge of the rugs, all
facing the altar, including GRIESHA's small pair.*

This is their Gurdwara, their temple.

*The voice-over is intimate,
like someone whispering in your ear.*

Behind a gauze, in a dream.

>   GRIESHA v.o.
>   (*Running over the hill.*)
>   Barbra!!

>   BARBRA v.o.
>   I love this time of day.

>   ANNIE v.o.
>   (*Whispers.*) Sorry we're late.

~~~~

>   LOVELEEN v.o.
> Brother, do you think we'll ever see a real Gurdwara?

GURJIT v.o.
God is in your heart, Loveleen.
My Gurdwara is as big as this orchard.
My love as deep, for both are infinite.

We imagine the family, YASH and PETER, listening to KESUR recite from the holy book. Perhaps leaves blow across the empty stage.

Act Four. Scene One.

> *The Basran Living Room. Early October, 1974. Six weeks later.*
>
> *The house is almost empty. The windows are boarded up. There are no pictures on the walls. A few objects are piled in the middle of the room for selling. Boxes and suitcases are by the door. DONNA[38] and YEBI pack boxes.*

GURJIT: (*Offstage.*) Thank you my friends. Until we meet again.

MICHAEL: Please let's have a toast. A small glass. Some champagne before everyone leaves. I insist. Anyone? (*Beat.*) I should have picked out a cold bottle. (*Calling outside to the pickers.*) Ladies and gentleman! Who would like a glass of sparkling champagne? Anybody? One tiny glass to celebrate. (*Pause.*) Yash, I know you can't resist a free drink.

YASH: Why not.

MICHAEL: Good man.

YASH: Here's to staying behind!

MICHAEL: Is that a smile I see? Yash, you devil!

> *They drink. YASH spits it out.*

YASH: Pft! Where'd you get this?

MICHAEL: The liquor store.

YASH: It's disgusting.

MICHAEL: Cold in here today. Stoves weren't lit.

YASH: Why bother? No one lives here anymore.

---

38   Donna is three months pregnant. Some people know, others don't.

MICHAEL: Yash please, if I could, one toast. To new partnerships. I couldn't manage this property without you.

YASH: It's warm for October. Good building weather.

MICHAEL: You keep an eye on those peach trees. Keep us in that land freeze and the government off our backs.

PETER enters.

PETER: I can't find my boots. (*Calling offstage.*) Annie they're not in here!

MICHAEL: Ah ha, the eternal student! Back to your intellectual habitat. I bet India will throw a parade. "Now the revolution can begin!"

PETER: Very funny. (*Keeps looking for his boots.*) You know we most likely will never meet again. Can I give you some advice? You have a habit of making these sweeping statements. It's very off-putting. Cut it down. Build it up. Embrace the RV Nation. You should learn the art of subtlety. That being said: I don't mind you. You have a good soul, I can see that much.

MICHAEL: Well thank you, thank you my friend. Thank you for everything. Subtly speaking, it's an *Agricultural* RV Park. But that was very… here.

MICHAEL hands PETER some bills.

PETER: What's this?

MICHAEL: For you.

PETER: (*Firmly.*) I don't want it.

MICHAEL: Don't be ridiculous. I know you don't have anything.

PETER: Actually I do. I've been tutoring all summer. (*Calling offstage.*) What I don't have are my boots…!!

BARBRA enters.

BARBRA: For God's sakes, take them!

BARBRA throws a pair of boots into the room and exits.

PETER: You're angry at me *again?!* (*Beat.*) (*Calling offstage.*) Barminder, these aren't my boots!

MICHAEL: Last spring I planted twelve acres of alfalfa. From that, I cleared four thousands dollars. Four thousand! What I'm trying to say is, I'm offering to lend it to you, 'cause I'm able to do it. I may not know how to talk about money, but you don't have to snub me.

PETER: No thank you. I said no thank you sir. If you offered me two hundred thousand dollars, I would still say no. This thing that you hold so dear, it has no power over me. Because my stock is in humanity. And we are moving forward, rising towards a higher truth, a happier time. And I am on the ground floor.

MICHAEL: And will you get there?

PETER: I hope so. Or show others the way.

MICHAEL: All these years, we've tried to outwit each other. And now the time has come to say goodbye. Well my friend, thank you. Now the earth can continue to turn. Did you hear, Gus got a job at the bank. I wonder if he'll last?

GURJIT: (*Offstage.*) Yes, thank you, thank you for everything.

BARBRA and YASH enter from outside.

BARBRA: (*Calling.*) The pickers are here to say goodbye!

YASH: Would it kill them to take a shower?

GURJIT enters from outside; he no longer wears a turban. His hair is cut short, his beard shaved. GURJIT looks at MICHAEL and PETER staring at him, as if they are his mirror. A stray hair is determined to keep sticking up, he tries to smooth it down.

After a moment, LOVELEEN enters from outside. She's been chasing after GURJIT all morning.

LOVELEEN: Gus…

GURJIT: Hurry up everyone.

ANNIE passes through.

ANNIE: Barbra, where are you?!

LOVELEEN: Gus please talk to me…

GURJIT: I'll be outside.

GURJIT goes outside. ANNIE exits to another room. LOVELEEN exits the same way. Chainsaws fire up in the background.

MICHAEL: Ah Yash! What do you think about adding three more blocks of trees down near the old pickers' cabins?

YASH: It'll be too cramped. The peaches need more sunlight than that.

MICHAEL: Who cares, we'll get the extra tax credit.

PETER: Nothing stands in the way of progress.

YASH: I said, forget it.

ANNIE enters.

ANNIE: Michael, the family is leaving at ten o'clock, yes?

MICHAEL: That's the plan, Anna Banana.

ANNIE: Mom asks if you could wait the extra fifteen minutes before chopping down her childhood orchard.

MICHAEL: Yes of course. What was I thinking, ah, not at all apparently… these farm guys…! (*Bleating like a goat.*) Meeeeh!

>   MICHAEL *runs outside.*

ANNIE: Did someone take grandpa to the hospital?

PETER: Yash said Gurjit took him this morning.

ANNIE: (*Accusing.*) Did he?

YASH: (*Accusing.*) Do you think I'm lying?

YEBI: (*Smiling.*) Kesur. Our resilient old Kesur. Speaking candidly, I think he's beyond repair. Or to put it more delicately, the apple must leave the tree eventually. As for me, I can only envy him.

>   YEBI *squashes a box. We hear glass break.*

Ah ha! Another point of proof! I should have guessed it.

YASH: Yebi strikes again.

>   YEBI *and* YASH *exit.* PETER *and* ANNIE *are finally alone.*

PETER: Annie… it's not too late. We could accomplish so much together.

ANNIE: Peter…

PETER: Don't waste your potential Annie. People are discussing things that will change India forever. We could be part of something.

ANNIE: I can't.

PETER: Look, I've been saving up all summer. If it's about money… Come to India with me. Come home.

ANNIE: I've been going over and over it in my head and, I'm gonna do it. I'm gonna build a Gurdwara. Right here. In town.

PETER: Did you get the permits?

ANNIE: City hall turned down the application. But I will convince them and raise the money and when it's finally done... our first Gurdwara, Peter.

PETER: Is this about Barminder?

ANNIE: This is about all of us. A better world is coming, Peter. I can see it.

PETER: And will you get there?

ANNIE: (*Firmly.*) Yes.

BARBRA: (*Offstage.*) Annie!

ANNIE kisses PETER.

ANNIE: Go back to India. Don't burn the place down.

BARBRA enters. From another room in the house, DONNA enters and packs boxes.

BARBRA: Did big grandpa go to the hospital?

ANNIE: Yea, Yash took him.

BARBRA: (*Curtly.*) Well he forgot the letter for the doctor.

ANNIE: I can take care of it.

BARBRA: Don't bother. Where is Yash? His mother is here to bless the property.

BARBRA exits with ANNIE following behind. YASH enters.

YASH: (*Yelling after BARBRA.*) I told her I wasn't interested.

DONNA has been busying herself with luggage. Now they are alone.

DONNA: Will you look at me? Yash. *One* look.

YASH: Why are you still here?

DONNA: Excuse me? Why don't you say something kind. (*Beat.*) Won't you say anything?

DONNA goes to kiss him. He refuses her.

YASH: See you later then.

DONNA hangs herself on him.

DONNA: I loved you Yash.

YASH: Come on now. What's the point of crying. We had our fun, didn't we, peaches? It's time to work. So, so, pull yourself together.

DONNA: I am a delicate soul. I can still see you, can't I? Yash... I love you so much.

YASH: Shh. Someone's coming.

YASH and DONNA separate. GURJIT and ANNIE enter together.

GURJIT: Barbra, Susan from the church is here.

BARBRA enters from another room.

BARBRA: Already? I look like a mess.

ANNIE: She doesn't want to come in. Yebi, where are you?!

YASH: The tractor is leaving in ten minutes. Hurry up or you'll be walking.

ANNIE exits. LOVELEEN enters.

LOVELEEN: My brother. Your hair looks nice.

GURJIT: Well, I start at the bank on Monday.

LOVELEEN: It'll grow back.

GURJIT: Not at the bank. (*Beat.*) Well we'd better get moving. There isn't much time left. What is that fishy smell?

GURJIT looks directly at YASH. YASH exits, DONNA follows him. LOVELEEN and GURJIT are alone for a moment.

LOVELEEN: Yes all right. Goodbye dear house, old grandfather house!

ANNIE enters with luggage.

GURJIT: Indeed. Once this day is over, we'll be done with it. (*To ANNIE, sarcastic.*) We didn't need Michael to save the day. We had your mother!

LOVELEEN: Gus I'm sorry…

GURJIT: Yes. I think we can all breathe easier now.

LOVELEEN looks to ANNIE. The relationship is strained.

LOVELEEN: Annie, my darling, you're looking better. Before you were worried and upset. Now look, it's all settled.

ANNIE: It'll be different this time, mom. Won't it?

LOVELEEN: Of course, you'll finish your studies.

ANNIE: I'll read to you on autumn nights.

LOVELEEN: Yes my darling, we'll fall asleep in front of the fire. Whatever books you want. Yes, I promise. Oh, my beautiful daughter. Your eyes are gleaming like diamonds.

ANNIE: Are you going to be happy mom?

LOVELEEN: Yes.

ANNIE: Truly happy?

LOVELEEN: Yes. I can feel it… Life is beginning again.

CHARLIE enters with a swaddle of clothes. MICHAEL enters behind her.

And here comes Charlie!

ANNIE: You look handsome, Gus-Uncle.

GURJIT: Yes well... thank you.

CHARLIE: (*Talking to her swaddle.*) Hello little baby. (*CHARLIE makes the sound of a crying baby.*) Hush, hush. Be quiet now, no need to cry.

DONNA: (*Grabbing the bundle of clothes.*) Stop that.

> *PAUL bursts into the room, out of breath. CHARLIE collects her bundle and takes it into another room.*

GURJIT: Ah ha, another one to bid us adieu.

PAUL: Oh god. I need to... I can't keep up like I used to, that's for sure. Ah! Have to catch my breath. My friends – oh, could I get some water – I've come –

> *ANNIE exits to get water for PAUL.*

GURJIT: To ask for more money? Excuse me... I can't watch.

> *GURJIT exits.*

PAUL: No. Ah! Lallie hello. And you're here too. The big tycoon. Well that saves me a trip. Here, this is for you... four hundred dollars and the rest is on the way.

MICHAEL: Am I dreaming? You old horse! All right, where'd you get it?

PAUL: Ah well... god it's hot in here. Is it hot in here?

> *ANNIE gives PAUL a glass of water.*

Thank you. So the city comes to my place, and they said we don't want a communal mailbox, we want the whole damn property! They're building a post office! And for you Lallie. (*Gives her money.*) Those city hall guys see potential and they snatch it right up. Now I'm sorry but I have to press on. I'll see you again on Thursday.

LOVELEEN: Actually, we're about to leave. We're moving today.

PAUL: Today? (*He sees the boxes.*) Oh well... May God bless each one of us. (*Beat.*) Everything comes to an end eventually, eh? So when I meet my end, remember... "that man was a stallion. God rest his soul." Hot weather for October. Well... ah... Brenda sends her best.

PAUL exits.

LOVELEEN: And with that, I guess there's no more putting it off. Oh wait, there's two things. Grandpa, he has his appointment at the hospital –

ANNIE: We took care of it.

LOVELEEN: Oh good. Then second is our Barminder. She's grown thin, she weeps... Michael Lopakhin, I always thought one day I would give her to you. You always seem happier when she walks into a room and I know Barminder would be up for it. Take the leap and be done with it.

MICHAEL: Yes, you're right Miss Basran. I don't know myself why it's taken so long. I guess the timing never seems to... But let's do it. 'Cause once you're gone, I'm afraid I won't have the courage to go through with it.

LOVELEEN: Yes. Excellent! Congratulations! Annie, let's give them some privacy. (*Calling.*) Barminder?

ANNIE: (*Calling.*) Barbra! Stop whatever you're doing! Seriously. Like right now.

MICHAEL: Yes. Ok, ok, ok.

MICHAEL looks at his watch. While waiting, he finds a scarf in an open box and tries to wrap a makeshift turban on his head. It looks ridiculous but before he can take it off, BARBRA enters and pretends to look for something.

Ah, hello there.

BARBRA: So strange. I can't find it anywhere.

MICHAEL: Umm, what are you looking for?

BARBRA: I packed the boxes myself, and still I can't seem to find...

MICHAEL: So... where are you moving? Are you going with Annie or Peter?

BARBRA: Peter? Why would I go with him?

MICHAEL: Back to India.

BARBRA: No I'm going to be living with Susan, from the church. She has a basement apartment I can stay in.

MICHAEL: So. Life in this house is really over.

BARBRA: Really, where is that stupid thing... In the trunk maybe...

MICHAEL: Well, I'm going to Vancouver. I leave in the morning. I'll be gone all winter.

BARBRA: Oh. That's nice.

MICHAEL: Do you remember this time last year? It was freezing. I helped you bring in the firewood from the shed. Ahm...

BARBRA: Yes.

MICHAEL: Yes?

BARBRA: I remember.

MICHAEL: – and this family has been so kind to me.

BARBRA: Yes.

MICHAEL: – and *you* have. And I just wanted... to...

> *Long pause. LOVELEEN can be heard laughing in another room with DONNA.*

...to thank you for all your hospitality.

BARBRA: Of course.

They share a silence.

MICHAEL: They say it's gonna be a high of fifty-five today.

BARBRA: I haven't looked. Our thermostat's broken.

YASH: (*Offstage.*) Michael! Are you in there?

MICHAEL: Yes. I'm coming!

MICHAEL exits. BARBRA holds a bundle of clothes and sobs softly. ANNIE enters.

ANNIE: Yes… and…?

BARBRA indicates "No." YASH and PETER enter.

PETER: I'm afraid the time has come.

YASH: I hate to agree with the nerd, but he's right.

PETER: Is "Susan From Church" still here?

BARBRA: Knock it off, I'm going to live with her.

ANNIE: You mean *work* for her.

BARBRA: And Yash! How can you go along with this?

YASH: At least one of us will be here.

ANNIE: It's only twenty trees.

YASH: Twenty Basran trees. I can do this, Annie. I promise you.

Beat.

LOVELEEN: (*Offstage.*) Kids?!

YASH: Ladies and gentleman, if I may, I know I'm not one for speeches… But a toast!

ANNIE/PETER/BARBRA: No!

GURJIT: (*Offstage.*) Kids?!

GURJIT and LOVELEEN enter.

LOVELEEN: Well that's all of us.

YASH: A toast. A *last* toast. To this old house. That raised me. That watched over us as we grew.

GURJIT: For fifty years…

YASH: But would we throw a parade for a small house? Four walls and a discount roof?

For fifty years, you have nurtured this family to the max, lifted our wisecracks to their zenith, guarded our dreams as we slept. House, thank you. No, no, I have to speak the truth! Dear house… I salute you!! You got the job done, my friend.

Beat.

BARBRA: Yash, you're worse than uncle.

Everyone stifles a bittersweet laugh, except YASH.

GURJIT: Time to walk the plank, my boy.

YASH: I am silent.

They sit in silence. Pause. MICHAEL enters. YEBI trails behind him.

MICHAEL: Well. If I don't leave now, I'll miss my meeting. Yebi, there's a few more boxes there.

LOVELEEN: When we leave, there won't be a soul in this place. Just an empty shell.

MICHAEL: Until the spring.

LOVELEEN: Is the truck all packed?

YEBI: (*In a husky voice.*) Don't worry, Miss Basran. I took care of that.

LOVELEEN: Why are you talking like that?

YEBI: (*In a husky voice.*) Some water went down the wrong tube.

YASH: How are you still alive?

> *BARBRA picks up a shovel from a pile of boxes. MICHAEL pretends to be scared.*

MICHAEL: Ah stop! Help! Run for your lives!

PETER: Really, we should get going. Before it gets too hot.

ANNIE: Ah ha! Peter, your boots! They're so muddy. (*Tearfully.*) So many harvests in these dirty boots.

GURJIT: Forward pirates! One battle left.

> *MICHAEL starts the business of locking up the house.*

MICHAEL: Until next time then. Yebi, you need a ride into town?

YEBI: I was going to ride my bike – but yeah that might be safer.

> *YEBI and MICHAEL exit. The rest exit one by one...*

LOVELEEN: Yes, let's go.

PETER: Hello to the new life!

> *PETER exits.*

ANNIE: Goodbye old life. Old house...! (*To BARBRA.*) Goodbye.

ANNIE exits. BARBRA glances around the room, her emotions starting to get the better of her.

YASH: (*To BARBRA.*) Come on then.

YASH takes BARBRA out. LOVELEEN and GURJIT are left alone. It seems they have been waiting for this moment. GURJIT sobs quietly, so as not to be heard.

GURJIT: I think I'll sit down. For just a little longer. How much these walls have seen. So many things I never saw.

LOVELEEN: Gus, please… I did what I thought was right. I'm not strong like you. When they died…

ANNIE: (*Offstage.*). Mom!

PETER: (*Offstage.*) (*In Punjabi.*) ਆ ਜਾਓ ਚਲੀਏ। **(Come on, let's go!)**

LOVELEEN: I'm not staying. We'll do this, and then I have to leave. Tell Annie for me.

GURJIT: Lovely, you can't do this to Annie again. She needs a mother – (*Resigned.*) You'll go back to India then?

LOVELEEN: Yes.

GURJIT: What happened to you, Lallie? I see you, and I don't know who you are anymore. What you did…

Beat.

This one hair keeps sticking up.

LOVELEEN: Griesha's hair did that too. (*She licks her hand and slicks it down.*) There. (*Beat.*) Good as new.

GURJIT: My dear, darling sister. (*Beat.*) I pray you find us again.

LOVELEEN: My brother, when did you grow up?

GURJIT: I don't know. (*Beat.*) I remember when I was five and you were eight, I'd sit right here and watch our mother open the gate. She'd unlock the shop, and you'd go running off to school. Life seemed warm then.

LOVELEEN: This precious, beautiful… our orchard. My life, my youth, my happiness… goodbye.

ANNIE: (*Offstage.*) Mom!?

PETER: (*Offstage.*) Hello!?

ANNIE: (*Offstage.*) Peter's driving the tractor!

LOVELEEN: Coming!

They exit. The sound of doors being locked. The tractor and voices grow distant, as they move into the orchard.

KESUR appears with an axe in hand. In the distance, the dull thud of an axe on a tree.

KESUR: Hello? Hello?! Left without me. And Gurjit forgot his wool coat. I know he takes his light one. All right then. (*He sits.*) The body gets tired. I think I'll rest a little. Waheguru.

The sound of trees, breaking and falling.

I can hear my bones cracking now.

CHARLIE enters, getting ready to hunker down for a winter inside the house. She sees KESUR.

CHARLIE: Come on, old friend.

KESUR: Griesha? Griesha, is that you? Home from your travels?

CHARLIE: No no, Kesur. It's me. Charlie.

KESUR: My life has gone by and what have I done?

> *They sit. The sound of trees breaking and falling.*

Silly fool. No strength, no strength…

> *Pause. Suddenly the door unlocks. ANNIE, PETER, YASH and MICHAEL come rushing in.*

ANNIE: Grandpa, we're/so sorry!

YASH: Sorry about that, old man.

KESUR: No need to/fuss.

ANNIE: (*To MICHAEL.*) How/could you?!

KESUR: (*To PETER.*) It doesn't matter.

YASH: (*To MICHAEL.*) Can you check the house/before you lock people in it!?

PETER: Let's get you in the/truck.

MICHAEL: My mistake! My mistake!

ANNIE: Goodbye house!

> *KESUR, ANNIE, PETER and YASH all exit. MICHAEL and CHARLIE stare at each other for a moment. Then MICHAEL exits. CHARLIE is left alone inside the house. Doors lock again, the truck doors slams, vehicles drive away.*
>
> *Lights and music begin to shift.*

Epilogue.

> *CHARLIE goes to the small house made of building blocks, which sits on a mound of dirt. She dismantles it. She scoops up the dirt and sprinkles it on the bare stage as she speaks.*

CHARLIE: My káwa told me a story once... Before there was an orchard here, before there was a ranch, there was a hill. And at the bottom of the hill... the Great Creek. Filled with the biggest sockeye salmon in the entire Okanagan. In the summer, the creek used to run red with fish, bursting out of the water and overflowing onto the rocks. My great-grandfather was the Salmon-Chief. People may come and go from this land. But the salmon is my brother and I belong to this creek.

> *A faint amber light streams though the once-locked door, next to ANNIE's room. It's a little boy's room, half packed away into boxes.*

GRIESHA v.o.: (*Whispers.*) And what happens next Charlie? Where will you go?

CHARLIE: I'll be *right here.*

> *Charlie sings three verses of the "Women's Warrior Song,"[39] filled with melancholy and resilience. It starts quietly and grows into a loud, defiant cry.*
>
> The End.

---

39 The "Women's Warrior Song" is a prayer song, received by Martina Pierre of the Lîlwat Nation thirty years ago during a sweat. The song is always to be sung for strength – never in anger. At the time of publishing the song was often sung in honour of the many missing and murdered Indigenous women.

Afterword:
Re-imagining Canadian History

By Sarena Parmar

How is a nation's identity formed? How is our history reflected back to us? In media? In the classroom? Through the social consciousness? Growing up, I was led to believe that old stock Canadians were historically European. When I closed my eyes, I saw the iconic "rural Canadian farmer." He was definitely white.

But immigrants of colour are always just getting here, always just arriving off the boat, no matter what decade we live in. *These* immigrants are *new*, they live in cities, they have accents. We fondly refer to them as New Canadians. And there is no alternative narrative. Oh, how wrong I was. I only had to look at my own family history.

This may not be your typical playwright's afterword, but more an essay, some academic, some personal, about the cultural tensions and history that influence the characters in this play. The Okanagan Valley is a beautiful and unlikely microcosm for the hidden multicultural history present in so many farming communities. I grew up in the Okanagan. On a fruit orchard. I am a third-generation Canadian. Let me tell you about where I come from...

While travelling through the Okanagan Valley in 1890, Lord and Lady Aberdeen were charmed by the mild climate and beauty of the picturesque valley. They bought the Coldstream Ranch and transformed it into a fruit orchard. Upon returning to England, the Aberdeens launched a recruiting campaign to lure "the right sort of immigrant" to the Okanagan, complete with glossy brochures. Lady Aberdeen extolled fruit ranching as the most civilized form of agriculture. And Governor Grey deemed horticulture as a natural fit for the Englishman of "refinement, culture, and distinction." The Okanagan Valley, with its new aristocratic aura, became a fashionable destination for British immigrants; and so, a primarily British class of "gentleman fruit ranchers" was established in the Okanagan.

Let us jump ahead. My family immigrated from India to the Okanagan in 1967. My grandmother's brother, who already lived in Westbank, sponsored my grandparents and their children. My grandparents worked at the lumber mill and Bylands Nursery. Three years later they bought our family orchard in Kelowna, BC. They worked their regular jobs during the day and farmed in the evenings. There was a lot of hard work, early mornings and manual labor, but the orchard was always a place of family and laughter. Eventually they opened a fruit stand, which is where I worked as a child.

In terms of ethnic demographics, not much had changed since the Aberdeens in 1890. In 1971, the population of the Central Okanagan was 50,180. According to the Canadian census, 26,300 identified as British. Other major groups were German, Scandinavian, and French. In Kelowna, 95% of the population was Caucasian, and 5% were Other. The Others included people of Japanese, South Asian, and Indigenous heritage. There were 120 Japanese, five "Negros," and no designated category for South Asians. But my mother tells me there were four South Asian families, including ours.

Growing up in a small community, there was no one outside our own family to share cultural customs; assimilation happened quickly. This tension created some unlikely misfits. The Japanese boy who dreams of being a cowboy, the First Nations woman who rode the rodeo better than any rancher, and South Asian farmers who were as North American as Johnny Appleseed. The erased pioneers, who paved the way for a multicultural Canada.

So who were these Outsiders?

A small Japanese community had been in the Okanagan since 1907. They lived side by side with fellow residents, many of them working in agriculture. But in 1942 everything changed; after the attack on Pearl Harbor, the federal government forcibly removed all Japanese-Canadians from the west coast, placing them in internment camps. Meanwhile, Okanagan fruit farmers, who were in desperate need of labour, requested that some Japanese be brought to the Valley to work, under the condition that all Japanese were removed once the war had ended. With anti-Japanese hysteria rising, internees were greeted by signs like "Coast Japs are not wanted. Get out!" The Japanese provided involuntary farm labour, until the last internment camp closed in the Okanagan in 1947. Despite intimidation from the government and locals to relocate east of the Rockies, many Japanese families stayed in the Okanagan. They bought orchards and continue to be an integral part of the Okanagan fruit farming community.

The Syilx People of the Okanagan Nation have always had a visible presence in the Okanagan, largely because the Westbank Reservation is located within Kelowna city limits, containing 5,340 acres of land. The Syilx respect four Food Chiefs, who symbolize their traditional diet: Saskatoon Berry, Bear, Bitterroot, and Salmon. The wild horse is also an inseparable part of Syilx culture, built on mutual respect. Over time ceremony and medicines were developed to honour and doctor the horse. As Europeans began to settle the region, they brought with them ranching and the rodeo, and the icon of the Cowboy. "Because of their long and rich relationship with the horse, the Okanagan community took naturally to the rodeo, horse racing, and trick riding, and helped develop these sports. Many became rodeo champions and successful ranchers," says Bill Cohen. I always found it cheeky that the Syilx people were riding horses before ranchers were on the scene. The Syilx were cowboys before there was a name for it. And proudly refer to themselves as Indian Cowboys.

While speaking with the facilitator of the Sncewips Heritage Museum, she said, "there are some (stories) I can tell you, and some I cannot." I think that encapsulates my journey of writing Charlie, the First Nations character. Charlie is experiencing another layer of narrative that is beyond my cultural access, which is why she remains rightly mysterious in my mind's eye and thus, in the play. There are some stories Charlie can tell us, and some she cannot.

The facts and numbers are much more scarce about South Asians in the area, for the simple truth that they're weren't very many. Maybe my family should have written it down, maybe that is what I have tried to do with this play. In some strange way, I'm trying to document the history of Punjabis in the Okanagan.

And then, similar to Chekhov's *Cherry Orchard*, Canada experienced a major change. In 1971, Prime Minister Pierre Trudeau passed the Multiculturalism Act and shortly after introduced immigration reforms, no longer limiting the number of immigrants from "undesirable countries." Without restrictions based on race, visible minorities steadily emigrated to Canada, changing the face of the country forever. The first Gurdwara, a Sikh temple, opened in Kelowna on May 30, 1982. There were 34 families.

But in the Okanagan, like most agricultural communities, there was a dichotomy. By necessity the community must band together. There is a reason why barn raising is a party; it takes many people. But there is also an underlying tension. The Outsider is always reminded of their place. The reminder gets subtler as the years go on. But that gentle reminder is still here today. I urge you, dear reader, to look for it.

Today the Kelowna I knew has changed greatly. The South Asian population has grown exponentially. There is a new Gurdwara with beautiful windows and domed sanctum – I got married there; the Okanagan Nation Alliance is bringing back the salmon through its hatchery program, and this year we sell our family orchard.

The way I grew up has almost disappeared. Our last ties to India, our agricultural roots, are about to be severed. I proudly know how to country two-step and drink a Budweiser, and I have fond memories of my aunts vacuuming the carpet of our old Gurdwara before my family hosted the "harvest celebration." I am a proud misfit.

So who is allowed to tell which stories? Who decides Canadian history?

A final thought. One of my fondest memories of *The Orchard* was during a performance at the Shaw Festival. A Sikh couple sat in the front row. They were in their 70s; the man was turbaned; they both wore karas. During Act Two, after the Basrans endure a racist attack, Kesur breaks the silence by explaining why we wear the kara:

KESUR: You know, I love this little bracelet. Do you know the first kara was made of simple iron, so every Sikh person could afford it. Cheap little thing. But when I see others wearing it, I remember: I am part of a big religion, a big group. And you all wear the kara too. Let me see.

LOVELEEN, GUS, ANNIE, BARBRA, and PETER all show their karas.

KESUR: So maybe here, the group is only us. But a small fry is still a potato.

As we all showed our karas onstage, the older gentleman gently touched his kara and quietly mumbled, "Yeah." I cannot describe what happened next. The air in the theatre changed. Because the play was performed in the round, the actors and the audience saw this otherwise invisible gesture. Suddenly people listened more closely. The actors playing Sikhs – some of us Sikh in real life – stood a little taller, a little prouder. I hope he did too. That is what theatre can do. Make the invisible seen.

> "...we are shown that it is through our power of speech
> and the larger unified voice of oral tradition
> that we exist as we do."
> —Sylix author, Arnie Louie

Farmers by Faith:
Following the Migrations of Sikh Cultivators

By Jagdeesh Mann

Early in the first act of *The Orchard*, family patriarch Kesur Basran stares out at the audience and defines his place in the world in two short declarative sentences.

"We come from Punjab, land of the five rivers, so green you can grow anything. We have been farmers since the birth of those five rivers," he proclaims, referring to his native state in North India which is also known as the breadbasket of the country.

It's the kind of self-affirming statement one can imagine Irish, Scandinavian, German and Ukrainian immigrant farmers making after finally arriving at their homesteads and being confronted by the vastness of Canada's Prairies.

In India, cultivating and living close to the land is integral to Punjabi identity. And land ownership has long been a source of social esteem for Punjabi Sikhs, whether they are living in India or abroad. The Punjabi word for landholder itself has an aristocratic history. Zameen means "land," and zameendar – literally means "of the land" – was a title once given to land owners who, a century ago in India, "owned" the soil, the minerals, the animals and the villages and even the peasants on their expansive holdings.

Today zameendars in India are mostly small plot holders, some holding fractions of acreages. But they still retain a sense of social prestige in states like Punjab, which remains primarily agrarian in economy with its population spread evenly across almost 13,000 villages comprised of a hundred to a few thousand people.

But when it comes to land ownership in Punjab, there is

an added deeper, almost transcendental, reverence for owning and working one's own plot. It is steeped in the Punjab's cultural psyche as articulated through Punjabi poetry, myth, and its spirituality.

The Sikh gurus hail from the Punjab, a region named for cradling five major river systems (*Panj* means five in Persian and *ab* means water). The hymns of Guru Nanak and the other nine Sikh prophets are rich with farming metaphors. These mystical stanzas speak about the virtues of honest labour (*kirt kamayee*), and of reaping karmically what one sows. Guru Nanak, the founder of Sikhism, the world's fifth-largest religion today, himself tilled the fields around Kartarpur in his latter years where he settled a religious community.

But over these past five decades, farming families in Punjab have struggled mightily. Market pressure on these small land holdings have squeezed and uprooted households. This has led to Punjab's farming families increasingly migrating overseas. They have resettled in countries like Canada, US, UK, Italy, Spain, and Australia, where many have chosen, in specific regions, to re-establish pastoral lives centred on farming. Starting in small waves as early as the 1900s, pioneering Sikhs migrants established colonies in Malaysia, Singapore, Kenya, and the US.

In Singapore today, for example, some of the city's most valuable parcels of land in its urban core were a century earlier home to numerous Sikh families and their dairy farms. And in California's Central Valley, situated from Yuba City to Bakersfield, the descendants of pioneering Sikh families today own vast acreages of peach orchards, nut groves, berry fields, and vegetable farms in the region.

In Canada, Sikhs have been farming parts of its rich Fraser Valley for over a century. But it has only been since the 1970s that a new wave of Sikh immigrants moved into the Okanagan and Similkameen Valleys in the province's interior.

These two neighbouring regions are renowned for their fruit orchards and vineyards. As you drive through the Crowsnest Highway that ribbons along the Canada-US border, and as you enter the outskirts of the Similkameen town of Keremeos, you will encounter countless roadside fruit and vegetable stalls bearing common Punjabi surnames like Brar, Sidhu, Mann, Gill, and others owned by Punjabi families.

Sarena Parmar, the playwright of *The Orchard*, grew up in the Okanagan in one such immigrant Punjabi Sikh household. Her family farm produced apples, pears, nectarines, peaches, apricots, and cherries. Depending on the season, various members of her extended multi-generational family pitched in at pruning, picking, tending, moving sprinklers, and attending the fruit stand.

While it was a bucolic existence – ebbing and flowing with the seasons – it suffered all the hardships of immigrant and farming life. The adults worked day jobs to counter unpredictable farming income, diseases and pests could wipe out an entire harvest, and while the fruits of their orchard were always within the reach of their hands, the ultimate "fruits" of their labours were always at the whims of market prices far beyond their grasp. And adding to all the vicissitudes of agrarian life was the racism and alienation these farming migrants first encountered from previous settled descendants of European migrants.

But for Parmar the memories that are most vivid are a childhood spent playing in the family orchard, and of the daily routines: the rich scent of morning tea, lunches of paranthas and homemade yogurt, evenings during the busy season when family and relatives would rest after long days, conversations flowing late into the summer nights.

"Canada in the 1970s brought the multicultural beginning of the Multiculturalism Act, and the lifting of restrictions off immigration from Asian countries. This led to a huge influx of immigrants from India who went on to change the social fabric of Canada," Parmar has been quoted as saying about this pivotal period in Canadian history.

Despite the hardships of early pioneer families, increasing numbers of Punjabi Sikh immigrant families have not been deterred from buying more orchards and holdings in BC's Agricultural Land Reserve and from rejuvenating the ailing family farm enterprise, long abandoned by the locals.

These families are cultivating small acreages in growing numbers, one of the few places in the West where family farms are growing in number and not being amalgamated into sprawling corporate enterprises. These family farmers are selling their produce farm-to-table via local community markets, and they are demonstrating, through their devotion to a traditional agrarian way of life, that the 'things' which bring meaning to our lives cannot always be priced by market forces.

Ultimately the story of Sarena Parmar's own family, and that of the fictional Basrans in her play, like other small acreage family farmers in BC, is as Canadian as that of the traditional prairie family wheat farmer standing firm against the giant combines of industrial-scale farming closing in around him.

But in this case the Punjabi Sikh farmers are not yielding ground and are quite content to keep farming as their previous forefathers and foremothers did for centuries, only halfway around the globe from their native Punjab region. It's that sense of history that makes these family farmers who they are, a nearly immovable presence once they are firmly planted, and allies to an older, slower way of life many of us in cities find ourselves yearning for.

Hard not to cheer for that.

Jagdeesh Mann is a journalist based in Vancouver, Canada. Twitter: @jagdeeshmann

Translation vs Transportation: Can Chekhov Only Speak Russian?

By Tim Carroll

I've always been puzzled about how to do Chekhov in English.

More than once, I have taken a friend to see a production of, say, *Uncle Vanya*, and ended up explaining that, actually, there is more to it than just people sitting around being miserable when they aren't yelling at each other. I tell them about the time I saw Chekhov done by a Russian company, and I was blown away by all the passion and love on stage. "That's all right for *you*," they declare, "but I didn't see that show, did I?"

So what are we missing when we do it in English? Why does it always end up sinking into that clichéd 'Chekhovian' mood? I have talked to Russian speakers who tell me that there is no real hope of capturing the particular combination of casual, real conversation with achingly beautiful lyricism that makes the original texts so dazzling. But we can't seem to resist trying. There is clearly something in Chekhov's stories and characters that makes us want to bring them to our audiences; and, at the same time, there is something in the poetry and the life of these plays that disappears when we try. We know, of course, that there is no such thing as a perfect translation; but it can't only be that. The other problem, in my experience, is that when we watch and listen to a Chekhov play, it is so easy to feel distanced by the overabundance of names and references to places and social arrangements of which we know little or nothing.

These, then, are the two main obstacles to Chekhov really catching fire in the hearts and minds of an English-speaking audience: the fact that poetry, as Robert Frost said, is what gets lost in translation; and the difficulty of engaging with characters who all seem to have thirteen names and keep talking about how many *versts* they had to travel to attend the *zemstvo*. And these are the reasons why, first, the job of translating Chekhov has so often been given to poets; and, second, the action has often been transported to a new and hopefully more resonant setting. Thus, in an Irish setting, someone with a reassuringly simply name like Patrick might talk about how many *miles* it is to the *town hall*. In the case of both solutions, whether it succeeds depends on how well it is done; and that, in turn, seems to me to depend on how much of themselves the translator is willing to bring to the task. It doesn't do to be too faithful to the original: if the new version is going to stand on its own feet, it has to be free to go for a walk on them, too.

I had been pondering all these questions for years, including while directing my own version of *The Seagull* in which every scene was improvised afresh each night by a different cast, when Sarena Parmar came to me with the idea to recreate *The Cherry Orchard* in the Okanagan Valley. I was immediately struck by the beautiful boldness of this idea. On the one hand, it had very clear parallels with the original play: the basic situation, of a family being forced by dwindling circumstances to sell off the land to which they are emotionally attached, was the same in both plays. Many of the characters, too, could be lifted across from 19th-century Russia to 20th-century Canada very easily: the ardent student, the dutiful daughter, the feckless father figure, and so on. And there were shared themes, especially the clash between an older generation with outdated but attractive attitudes and a younger one with manners which might be brash and unappealing but who get things done.

And yet, at the same time, I was taken aback by the obstacles Sarena was throwing in her own path. The most obvious was the immigrant context: while it has never occurred to the aristocratic family in *The Cherry Orchard* that they might have to leave one day, the family in Sarena's *Orchard* has always known that their toehold in the new country is precarious. This changes a great deal about the plot, and has a particularly strong impact on the character and actions of the mother. Above all, the immigrant family version brings race divisions into the equation. In Chekhov, the great divider is class: in Parmar, the addition of race complicates the picture in so many ways one would not dare to start listing them. But it's not just one layer of racial complexity: Sarena's desire to portray the multiplicity of backgrounds one might find in the Okanagan gives us not just Sikhs and white Canadians, but First Nations people and even people of Japanese descent – perhaps interned or the children of internees in British Columbia during the Second World War. Everyone in the play is trying to discover and negotiate their place in a complicated pecking order that operates within and between ethnic groups. And then Sarena, in true Chekhovian fashion, adds the greatest complicator of them all: love.

Can any play hold all these levels of meaning and perspective? There were times, I am sure, when Sarena wondered if she had tried to cram too much in. But the play, however multi-layered it might be, landed very directly on its audience: they may not have known any more about Sikhs in British Columbia than they did about faded aristocrats in Russia, but the very fact of its being set in Canada challenged them to see it as part of their own story, as of course it is. I think it was a challenge which they felt honoured to accept. For the rest, the direct sincerity of Sarena's language, and her personal investment in what was unmistakably a labour of love, created a powerfully moving theatre experience of which we were all very proud.

Tim Carroll (a.k.a. tc) is a renowned theatre and opera director with over 25 years of experience worldwide. He is the current Artistic Director of the Shaw Festival.

Journey of the Kishu-Ben Dialect: Alternate Japanese Translation

Translated by
Chuck Tasaka,
Mayumi Takasaki and
Carolyn Nakagawa

This dialect of Japanese was spoken by Japanese Canadian families who immigrated to Steveston, BC prior to World War II, a fisherman's dialect that originated in the Wakayama prefecture of Japan (known as Kishu-ben).

This particular dialect has become a unique time-capsule. Some aspects of the language have become antiquated, preserved by the community from the time of their emigration. And in other ways, the dialect has evolved as it settled into its new Canadian homeland. Embedded in the "Steveston-Ben" dialect are hybrid words of English and Japanese that have taken on their own meaning and nostalgia. There are straightforward terms like "furendo" meaning friend, or "no-guru" meaning no good. And more complex terms like "hai-kara," meaning high-collar; originally meant to describe Japanese naval offices in 19th-century Japan, due to their high stiff European collars. The phrase evolved to describe someone who is well-dressed, Westernized and pleased with themselves.

I hope you enjoy this rare translation. The work was facilitated by playwright and poet Carolyn Nakagawa; and led by Japanese-Canadian elders Chuck Tasaka and Mayumi Takasaki, who grew up in and around the Steveston community during that time. Although it is still spoken by some Nisei[40]

---

40 Second generation.

and Sansei[41] Japanese-Canadians, it is understood less and less with each generation.

Sarena Parmar, playwright of The Orchard (After Chekhov).

~

Excerpt from Act Three, Scene Two.

> *The party is in full swing. DONNA waltzes in, drunk and breathless from dancing. As the scene progresses, YEBI finds himself alone with DONNA for a moment.*
>
> *DONNA drapes herself on YEBI.*

YEBI: If I may, you might look on me like a spineless bug, and maybe you're right, but – stop that – I speak from the heart, and…

(*In Japanese.*) Sanae, me, yuu-kara-ne. Yuu-wa me-no muneh ni oo-kaze mitai-ni butsuketa yo! **(Senae, you have hit my heart like a big wind –)**

DONNA: Don't speak like that here.

YEBI: (*In Japanese.*) Sanae, yuu, honto-ni hana-takai-ne. Itsumo 'hai-kallaa' no kami shitelu-de. Yuu-no 'kimono' – Me, yuu-no 'fu-ren-do' daka-lah, kii-te, "Minna yuu o baka-ni shite-lu-yo." **(You stick your nose up. You wear you hair "high-collar"… your clothes – I tell you as a friend, Senae. People think of you as a fool!)**

> *YEBI pulls off DONNA's blonde wig.*

DONNA: I look like a fool?! (*In Japanese.*) You-wa, yoo yuu-te!! Ebi-saka no ebi. Ebi no 'kao-boi'! **(You, you have the nerve to say that?! Yebisaka, the shrimp! The cowboy shrimp.)**

---

41 Third generation.

YEBI: (*In Japanese.*) You, hakujin no Mae-de fuuwari koto suruna na. **(You… in front of white people, you have to watch yourself.)**

DONNA throws a glass of water at YEBI.

DONNA: No, no, I'm dreaming now.

YEBI: (*Sighs.*) (*In Japanese.*) Ah, sou yanou. "Misfortune"-san, ha-loo. Mou, tomodachi daka-lah, ee-kao shite-ageru yo. **(Ah I see… Hello "Mr. Misfortune." I almost welcome him with a smile.)**